EMPLOYM

MW00444372

Perils and Pitfalls of California Employment Law
A Guide for HR Professionals

MATTHEW S. EFFLAND

Society for Human Resource Management
Alexandria, Virginia
www.shrm.org

Strategic Human Resource Management India
Mumbai, India
www.shrmindia.org

Society for Human Resource Management
Haidian District Beijing, China
www.shrm.org/cn

The Society for Human Resource Management (SHRM) is the world's largest association devoted to human resource management. Representing more than 250,000 members in over 140 countries, the Society serves the needs of HR professionals and advances the interests of the HR profession. Founded in 1948, SHRM has more than 575 affiliated chapters within the United States and subsidiary offices in China, India and United Arab Emirates. Visit SHRM Online at www.shrm.org.

Interior and Cover Design: Auburn Associates, Inc.

Library of Congress Cataloging-in-Publication Data
Effland, Matthew S., author.
  Perils and pitfalls of California employment law : a guide for
  HR professionals / Matthew S. Effland.
    pages   cm
  Includes bibliographical references and index.
  ISBN 978-1-58644-363-4
  1. Labor laws and legislation—California. I. Title.
  KFC556.E34 2014
  344.79401—dc23
                          2014016022

Ogletree Deakins/SHRM
Employment Law Series
Series Editor: Jathan Janove

Give Your Company a Fighting Chance: An HR Guide to Understanding and Preventing Workplace Violence
by Maria Greco Danaher

Perils and Pitfalls of California Employment Law: A Guide for HR Professionals
by Matthew S. Effland

Contents

Prologue

Los Angeles, November 2011

"It can't really be *that* bad."

The voice of my client's vice president of human resources came over the telephone's speaker, and I closed my eyes and sighed. Quietly. This wasn't the first time (or the 15th) that I'd heard such a statement since moving to California.

"I guess it depends on how you define 'bad,'" I responded. "Employment litigation in California *is* different—the state statutes allow more damages than the federal statues, which is why the plaintiff filed in state court. And, since the state statutes allow for individual liability, she sued the assistant manager personally, meaning we can't remove the case to federal court. There are no caps on damages, so million-dollar verdicts are not unheard of—which explains why Plaintiff's opening settlement demand was so high. The civil litigation rules here are set up to encourage court hearings on almost any dispute that arises, meaning the cost of pre-trial litigation is going to be significantly higher than what you're used to. And, while judges will usually kick one or two of the claims a plaintiff brings, full dismissal short of trial is rare, meaning plaintiff attorneys will work the heck out of cases with the hope of driving up the cost of settlement."

"But we didn't do anything wrong!" The frustration in her voice was clear.

"I know," I said, trying to sound soothing. "There's a reason companies think long and hard about moving to—or staying in—California. The legal landscape is terrifying—but your business makes money, right?"

"Our revenue is 125 percent of what was expected," she acknowledged. "There is a lot of business to be had between our LA and San Francisco operations."

"Exactly—you're here because business is very good," I said. "The litigation—and potential exposure—are just unfortunate costs of getting that increased business."

Silence . . . and then it was the VP-HR's turn to sigh. "OK," she said. "So what do we do now?"

⚖️ ⚖️ ⚖️

At the time I moved to Los Angeles from the Midwest, I had already practiced for more than 10 years. I'd tried cases, argued appeals, and counseled numerous clients on the intricacies of federal employment law. When the opportunity arose to help grow our LA office, I couldn't pass it up. After all, I'd grown up in Simi Valley (a suburb of Los Angeles), was comfortable with the southern California lifestyle, and was, quite frankly, tired of shoveling snow. Sure, I'd heard the horror stories about how difficult California employment laws were, but the cynic in me figured it was an exaggeration.

So, I took a short sabbatical, studied for my first bar exam in over a decade, and packed up my family for the 2,000-mile move to the Golden State. My first day in the LA office, after unpacking the pictures of my kids and setting out the signed Magic Johnson basketball I'd carried for years as a lifelong LA Laker's fan, I agreed to help one of my partners—who was swamped preparing for a federal hearing—with a discovery motion. This motion was a garden-variety filing that you see in almost every litigation matter, asking the court to increase the total number of interrogatories—written questions that the other party has to answer under oath. No big deal, I thought; I'd drafted many such motions over the years.

I got to work by pulling up a previous discovery motion filed in the case to use as a template. Immediately I was taken aback by the format of the motion—it looked really strange. The more I read, the stranger it looked. Among other things, it was three times longer and included a lot more detail than any comparable motion I'd seen.

Most confusing of all was that the motion was titled "Ex Parte Motion for Relief." Now, I'd been to law school and knew very well what "ex parte" meant—literally it means "for one party." Practically, it means one lawyer is talking to a judge about a case without the other side's lawyer present, and it is one of those basic things lawyers are not supposed to do. Completely confused at this point, I took advantage of the most valuable resource any attorney has—I asked my secretary.

"Liz," I said, trying my best to sound casual. "I'm working on this discovery motion, and just had a quick question about this whole 'ex parte' thing . . ."

Thus began my journey into the byzantine, contentious, and, for clients, incredibly expensive world of California employment law and litigation.

⚖️ ⚖️ ⚖️

December 2013

Looking back, I still shake my head at the learning experience. Whether it was dealing with ex parte motions (which, incidentally, means running to court to get a quick decision with *very* little notice to the other side), learning the difference between the FEHA (California's Fair Employment and Housing Act) and the CFRA (the California Family Rights Act) and how those laws differ from Title VII and the Family and Medical Leave Act, or coming to terms with the fact that litigation in California regularly costs two to four times what it does anywhere else, I now had a first-hand understanding of just how "different" the practice of law was in California.

The lessons, painful as they were to experience, were at the same time helpful to my practice. I was in a solid position to help counsel my clients, and the clients of other attorneys in my firm, who were stepping into the whirlpool of California employment law for the first time. As our Los Angeles office grew, and as more and more national clients engaged our west coast services, I realized just how much of a disconnect exists between those who work in HR and employment law in California and those who do so everywhere else. I was also able to see, first hand, the damage caused to businesses that did not have sufficient appreciation for the unique burdens California law places on businesses within the state.

In this book, I have tried to summarize the key *substantive* employment laws of California and discuss the ways in which they most differ from the federal statutes that guide most of the rest of the country. It does not discuss every law, or even every difference in the laws that are discussed—such a treatise (and they do exist) would be hundreds of pages long and involve nearly as many exceptions as rules. But what I *have* done is approach this book from the perspective of an experienced HR professional who finds himself or herself tasked with managing a workforce in California for the first time. I imagine such a person asking some basic questions, like:

- How do California's wage and hour laws compare with the federal Fair Labor Standards Act (FLSA) standards?
- How is overtime treated? And are my exempt employees from elsewhere also exempt in California?
- Do I need to amend my discrimination policies?
- Are the risks of violating the harassment laws greater in California than elsewhere?
- Are the rumors I've heard about employees getting months and months of protected leave from work true? (Spoiler Alert: Yes.)
- What about California's famous privacy rights? Medical marijuana laws? Background check limitations? And so on . . .

To answer these questions, I've divided this book into five primary chapters. The first two chapters deal with the most fundamental of issues—what it means to be an "employee" in California, and how you schedule and pay employees.

I turn next to a discussion of the requirements found in California's primary anti-discrimination and harassment statute, the FEHA, and how it significantly expands the rights of employees well beyond what is found in the various federal employment laws (Title VII, the Americans with Disabilities Act, or ADA, and the Age Discrimination in Employment Act, or ADEA).

I then discuss California's numerous leave of absence laws. The state goes far beyond anything the federal government requires and provides a dozen different forms of protected leave. In addition to discussing the specifics of the different leave laws, Chapter 4 offers suggestions on how to effectively and legally manage your workforce in the face of such laws by drawing on the knowledge of two experienced HR executives.

Finally, I conclude with a "day in the life" of a California HR director. Follow HR Manager Shelia on her journey through a typical, fun-filled day in the world of human resource management as she hits on many of the other laws that companies run into on a daily basis in the Golden State.

Whether you are contemplating a move to the state or are a life-long resident looking to brush up on the basics, I hope this book gives you some insight on how to navigate the complex and burdensome waters of California employment law.

Of course, while I sincerely hope this book provides you with helpful insight, *nothing in it is intended to constitute legal advice, and no one reading this book should construe it as such. Buying and reading this book does NOT create an attorney-client relationship.* If you believe you or your company is in need of management-side employment law advice, I strongly encourage you to put down the book and go hire a lawyer!

1

California Wage and Hour Law, Part I:

The World of the Wage Order

"Here be dragons." In medieval times, cartographers would use this warning label (or a picture of a ferocious dragon or slithering sea serpent) to denote uncharted—and presumably perilous—areas on a map. The phrase seems particularly appropriate for employers that are familiar with the landscape of federal requirements, and yet find themselves navigating the potentially treacherous waters of California law. It is primarily for this reason that I chose to start this book with a two-part discussion of California's wage and hour law.

Wage and hour law, in general, is very detailed, and very unforgiving. It was decided long ago in this country that one thing a company could never, ever mess with was a worker's pay. If someone performed work, that person had to be paid—no matter what. On the back of this most simple of propositions the federal government established an entire network of legal requirements and procedures—everything from overtime requirements to minimum wage to strict requirements for what type of employee qualified for a salary.

Perhaps not surprisingly, California added to the federal scheme over the years what it considers to be further, needed protections for the workers within its jurisdiction. In some ways, California's laws simply enhance the federal standards, like making overtime kick in after eight hours in a day, instead of after 40 hours in a week. In other ways, California goes well beyond the most aggressive efforts of the U.S. Department of Labor, such as creating a system that mandates suitable seating or imposing significant fines if pay stubs do not contain nine specific items of information.

To best explain the complex wage and hour requirements California places on businesses that operate within its state, I've chosen to approach the topic from the perspective of a company moving into the state. What are the differences an experienced HR manager needs to know to avoid trouble with the state Division of Labor Standards Enforcement (DLSE)? How much can one rely on a solid, even superior, knowledge of federal wage and hour law? (Hint: Not much.)

To this end, I start with a discussion of something unique to California: the Wage Orders. It is only through a basic understanding of these Wage Orders, and how they affect every aspect of employment in California, that someone can start to grasp just how complex doing business in the Golden State can be.

The Industrial Welfare Commission Wage Orders

A Brief History Lesson

The Industrial Welfare Commission (IWC) is the state agency empowered to regulate working conditions in California under Article XIV of the California Constitution. Established by the State Legislature in 1913, the IWC issued its first Wage Orders in 1916. The original Wage Orders regulated working conditions for women and children in various industries and established a statewide minimum wage (16 cents).

The legislature subsequently amended the California Labor Code in 1972 and 1973, expanding the IWC's authority to further include regulation of working conditions for men. The 1974 Wage Orders were the first ones applicable to *all* California employees.

The most recent series of amendments to the Wage Orders came in 2000. Among other things, these amendments implemented the Eight-Hour-Day Restoration and Workplace Flexibility Act of 1999 (A.B. 60), which took effect on January 1, 2000, and reinstated the requirement that employees receive daily overtime in addition to weekly. Since then, the Wage Orders have been republished to reflect increases to the minimum wage and updated to include other statutory changes.

Enforcement

Although the IWC was defunded effective July 1, 2004, the Wage Orders—18 in all—remain in full effect. The Division of Labor Standards Enforcement (DLSE) and the Labor Commissioner's Office are the state agencies now charged with enforcing the Wage Orders and the provisions of the Labor Code.

"Industry" and "Occupational" Orders

As a starting point, it's important to understand the various types of Wage Orders. Some are industry-specific whereas others apply to certain occupations. There is also a minimum wage Order applicable to almost *all* employees (with certain limited exceptions, such as outside salespersons, and employees who are parents, spouses, or children of the employer). Finally, there is a "catch-all" Wage Order, applicable to "Miscellaneous Employees" who are not otherwise covered by an industry- or occupation-specific Order.

Determining Which Wage Order Applies to You

Figuring out which IWC Wage Order covers your business's employees is not always easy. Each Wage Order (except the minimum wage Order) is numbered (1-17) and covers either an industry (Orders 1-3 and 5-13) or a set of occupations in industries not covered by other Wage Orders (Orders 4 and 14-17). As we mentioned above, there is also a "minimum wage" Order that is not associated with a number.

To identify the correct Wage Order(s) for your business, some initial questions to ask are below.

Is My Business Covered by an Industry Order?

First, you must identify the main function of your business to determine whether there is an Industry Order that fits your company's primary purpose. The Industry Orders are summarized in Table 1.1.

Table 1.1. Industry Wage Orders	
Industry	**Wage Order No.**
Manufacturing Industry	1-2001
Personal Service Industry	2-2001
Canning, Freezing, Preserving Industry	3-2001
Public Housekeeping Industry	5-2001
Laundry, Linen Supply, Dry Cleaning, Dyeing Industry	6-2001
Mercantile Industry	7-2001
Industries Handling Products After Harvest	8-2001
Transportation Industry	9-2001
Amusement and Recreation Industry	10-2001
Broadcasting Industry	11-2001
Motion Picture Industry	12-2001
Industries Preparing Agricultural Products for Market, On the Farm	13-2001

Is My Business Covered by More Than One Industry Order?

The industrial Wage Orders classify businesses based on the business's main purpose. Clearly, however, not all businesses are neatly categorized. A business with a variety of operations could seemingly straddle two (or even more) industries. In this scenario a reasonable employer will ask: *Which order applies?* Answer (as always): *It depends.* It can be difficult to fit unique and varied business structures into a limited set of categories. With that said, two types of business structures are most common—businesses with a "main" purpose that also have operations incidental to that purpose, and true "multipurpose" businesses.

Identifying the Primary Purpose of Your Business

When a business has an identifiable main purpose covered by an Industry Order, that single Order will apply. Moreover, if your business is covered by an Industry Order, the industrial Wage Order will apply to *all* of your employees. As an example, if you operate a fitness center in San Diego or a nail salon in Sacramento, all of your employees are covered by Wage Order 2-2001 (Personal Service Industry).

The applicable Industry Order covers all operations of your business even if your business also involves incidental operations that would seem to fall under another Order. An example: A California food manufacturer with its own deep freeze operation is entirely covered under Order 1-2001 (Manufacturing Industry) even though deep freeze operations are covered under Order 3-2001, which covers the Canning, Freezing, and Preserving Industry.

Identifying a True "Multipurpose" Business

The situation is different in the case of true multipurpose businesses. When a business has separate and distinct units, different Industry Orders cover those distinct units *if* they operate for different business purposes, *and* management is organized separately at all levels. Understandably, mixed-operation businesses can be headache-inducing for employers trying to determine the correct Wage Order coverage. The DLSE notes that these problematic determinations do not require an audit of company receipts to establish the principal business purpose. A broad assessment through observation and common sense, with appropriate guidance, is advisable here.

A multipurpose example: A major retail department store chain is covered by Order 7-2001 (Mercantile Industry). If, however, the department store chain also operates a restaurant at its San Francisco location, the restaurant clearly operates for a purpose different than the store's main purpose—retail sales. Assuming the restaurant's management is separately organized from store management, the restaurant's employees are covered by Order 5-2001 (Public Housekeeping Activities).

None of Our Operations Are Covered by an Industry Order. Now What?

What if none of the Industry Orders seem to apply to your business, and your business does not engage in any incidental activities that would fall under Order 5-2001? If that is indeed the case, you need to check the Occupational Wage Orders to see which Occupational Order(s) may apply to specific employees based on the work they perform. The Occupational Wage Orders are summarized in Table 1.2.

Employees who are not covered by one of the Wage Orders specific to an occupation are covered by Wage Order 17-2001 (Miscellaneous Employees), which the IWC has considered to be an occupational Wage Order.

Table 1.2. Occupational Wage Orders	
Occupation	**Wage Order No.**
Professional, Technical, Clerical, Mechanical, and Similar Occupations	4-2001
Agricultural Occupations	14-2001
Household Occupations	15-2001
On-Site Occupations in Construction, Drilling, Logging, and Mining Industries	16-2001
Miscellaneous Employees	17-2001

Understanding How the Wage Orders "Work"

It may help to think of the Industry Orders as "all-consuming" of that industry, whereas the Occupational Orders address specific jobs within industries not covered by specific Industry Orders. Of course, this is a bit of an oversimplification (of necessity).

A few examples may help shed light on the potentially confusing and complicated interplay of the Industry and Occupational Orders:

IWC Wage Order 1-2001 applies to an office worker in a manufacturing plant—for example, auto plant, lumber yard, or textile manufacturer—because that Order covers the manufacturing industry.

IWC Wage Order 4-2001 (Professional, Technical, Clerical, Mechanical, and Similar Occupations) applies to an office worker in an insurance company or law firm because those industries are not covered by industry-specific Orders.

The DLSE has published *Which IWC Order?*, which is a useful guide with an index of business and occupations and their corresponding Wage Orders.

Identifying Exempt Employees under the Wage Orders

Once you have successfully determined which Wage Order applies to your business and your employees, you will need to determine which, if any, of your employees are exempt from the Wage Order's application.

Like many aspects of California's wage and hour law, Wage Order exemptions are not always clear-cut. Certain individual occupations are expressly exempted from specified sections of the Wage Orders, so any applicable Order should be closely reviewed. In addition, if an employee is exempt from a Wage Order, the employee is not necessarily exempt from the California Labor Code provisions.

Below are some examples of the most common Wage Order exemptions an employer is likely to encounter. Let's dispense with an easy one at the outset—the Outside Salespersons exemption.

Outside and Inside Salespersons

Outside salespersons are explicitly exempt from *all* the Wage Orders. Each Wage Order defines an outside salesperson as someone who "customarily and regularly" works more than half of his or her workday away from the employer's place of business selling, obtaining orders, or securing contracts for goods, services, and anything in between. The key is the "more than 50 percent" factor—it is quantity rather than quality that controls.

Compare this exemption with the narrower exemption for inside salespersons: Inside salespeople do not receive a similarly wholesale exemption from the Orders. However, inside salespeople *are* exempt from the daily overtime and alternative workweek provisions of Orders 4-2001 (Professional, Technical, Clerical, Mechanical, and Similar Occupations) and 7-2001 (Mercantile Industry), *if* their earnings equal more than 1.5 times the minimum wage *and* more than 50 percent of their compensation comes from commissions. Again—read the Wage Orders carefully, and don't hesitate to seek legal advice in this area.

White-Collar Exemptions (Executive, Administrative, and Professional)

Employers outside of California are likely already familiar with the so-called white-collar exemptions under federal law. With the exception of Order 14-2001 (Agricultural Occupations) and Order 17-2001 (Miscellaneous Employees), each Wage Order similarly contains explicit Executive, Administrative, and Professional exemptions. Although the California exemptions are modeled largely on the federal white-collar exemptions, employers must be aware that there are important differences between these exemptions under California law, versus federal law.

How Are the White-Collar Exemptions
Similar under California and Federal Law?

Most importantly—whether under state or federal law—employers must bear in mind that these exemptions are defined by *law* (that is, by the Wage Orders or the applicable federal regulations). This means the employer and the employee cannot simply agree the employee's position is exempt or rely on the fact that it is designated that way. Basically, the rules are the rules, and the parties cannot try to contract around what the law requires.

Also under state and federal law, each of the white-collar exemptions has two components: a salary test and a job duties test. An employee must earn a certain minimum salary and have job duties that meet a certain test to qualify for the exemption.

How Are the White-Collar Exemptions
Different under California and Federal Law?

The short answer here is that *the salary test and the job duties test are different under state versus under federal law.* The minimum salary requirement for the white-collar exemptions under federal law is a bit lower than under state law—understandably so, considering that the federal minimum wage is lower than the minimum wage in California.

The more significant divergence—that is, the point of difference most likely to trip up an employer that is unfamiliar with the ins and outs of California's complex and often unique labor and employment laws—is found in the job duties test. In California, the test to determine whether an employee's job duties meet the requirements to qualify for a white-collar exemption is *not* the same as the job duties test under federal law. We will discuss this in more detail shortly.

Salary Test

Each white-collar exemption contains the same salary requirement, or "salary test." To qualify for any of the three exemptions, an employee must earn a monthly salary of at least two times the state minimum wage for full-time employment (40 hours/week). With the current $8.00 minimum wage in California, this means an exempt employee must earn a salary of *at least* $640.00 per week, or $2,733.33 per month,

CALIFORNIA EMPLOYMENT LAW FOR HR PROFESSIONALS | **9**

to pass the salary test in 2013. The federal exemptions require a minimum salary of $455.00 per week, or $1,972.00 per month to qualify.

The minimum monthly salary requirement to preserve an employee's exempt status under state law will increase to $3,120.00 per month as of July 1, 2014, when the state minimum wage rate goes from $8.00 per hour to $9.00 per hour. This amount will change again, to $3,466.67 effective January 1, 2016, when California's minimum wage increases to $10.00 per hour.

The Wage Orders also specifically exempt certain highly paid computer software employees based on wage rates (minimum hourly rate $49.77 required), and highly paid physicians and surgeons who are paid hourly.

Fee-Basis Employees

In contrast to salaried employees who receive a fixed compensation amount regardless of the number of hours worked, fee-basis employees receive a fixed sum for the performance of a single and unique job. (Employees who repeatedly receive the same amount for performance of an identical task on multiple occasions, however, will not be considered to work on a fee basis.)

The Fair Labor Standards Act (FLSA) contains exceptions to the salary basis test for professionals and administrative employees who are paid on a fee basis and who earn fees in an amount equal to or greater than the minimum weekly salary standard under federal law. Notably, California law does *not* provide for an equivalent exception. In other words, an employee who works for fees and does not receive a salary will not qualify for a white-collar exemption based on the salary test in California—even if the employee would otherwise qualify under state law.

Job Duties Test: A Completely Different Standard

After the threshold salary inquiry, employers must look to the type of work an employee is primarily engaged in to determine if that employee's job duties meet the requirements of an exemption. The Wage Orders stipulate that "primarily engaged in" means an employee must spend more than half of his or her work time performing exempt duties to qualify for one of the three exemptions. This standard may seem significantly different from the federal test. That is because it is!

The job duties test under California law is considered "quantitative" (in contrast to the federal "qualitative" test). That is, the Wage Orders define the work an employee is primarily engaged in based on a numeric analysis of the amount of time for which an employee is in fact performing exempt activities. Foremost in making this determination under the California job duties test, an employer must look at *how the employee actually spends his or her time* (which may differ dramatically from what a written job description establishes as the expected duties of the position).

In contrast, federal law asks what an employee's "primary duty" is, and is less concerned with ascertaining whether more than 50 percent of the employee's time is indeed occupied by exempt tasks. Thus, an employer does not necessarily have to get out a stopwatch when applying the federal test.

Of course, this difference between state and federal law need not always yield different results. In many cases, the result is the same. With that said, a California employer should proceed with caution in this area, especially with regard to any employees who may spend "about half" their time on exempt tasks. For such employees, a thorough analysis is necessary to determine whether *at least* 50.1 percent of the employee's time is occupied by exempt job duties. If not, the employee is *not* considered exempt under California law.

As under federal law, an additional requirement of each state exemption is that, to qualify, an employee must regularly exercise discretion and independent judgment in the performance of his or her job duties. Each Wage Order further specifies the type of work that qualifies an employee for each exemption. Detailed descriptions are available in the Wage Orders themselves. The Wage Orders actually refer to the equivalent exemption's specific federal code provisions (e.g., 29 C.F.R. §§ 541.207 and 541.301 et seq.) to help define the terms that describe these exemptions. With that caveat, it is probably helpful to provide a quick guide to the basics of the three exemptions.

Executive Exemption

Similar to the FLSA, to qualify for the Executive exemption the nature of the employee's job duties must involve managing the business or some department or subdivision thereof. Other requirements for this exemption under state law similarly mirror those under federal law.

Administrative Exemption

This exemption applies to certain administrative employees of a school system or educational institution, as well as to employees whose primary job duties consist of office work directly related to management policies or general business operations, of a business or of the business's customers. Like the Executive exemption, the requirements for the Administrative exemption under California law are much like those under the FLSA.

Professional Exemption

The standard that must be met for an employee to qualify for the Professional exemption is a bit more rigorous than either the Executive or Administrative exemptions. The details are too numerous to address here and would probably confuse more than clarify. For the most part, as with the Executive and Administrative exemptions, the requirements in this area are similar to those under the FLSA.

That being said—in only the most birds-eye view fashion—employers should note that to be considered an exempt professional an employee must either be licensed by the state of California to practice in the fields of law, medicine (with the exception of nurses and pharmacists), or other areas specifically enumerated in the Wage Orders, or the employee must be primarily engaged in a "learned or artistic profession." As the meaning of *this* phrase may not seem immediately clear, let's take a brief moment to examine how the Wage Orders define "learned" or "artistic" professions.

What Does It Mean to Be Engaged in a "Learned or Artistic Profession?"

The Wage Orders treat "learned" professions as those that customarily require advanced scientific or other knowledge, or prolonged instruction and study (as distinguishable from general academic education). A licensed CPA, for example, could meet this standard.

"Artistic" professions, by comparison, are those in which the work is original and creative, derived primarily from the employee's imagination, inventiveness, or talents, and intellectual and varied in character (as opposed to routine mental, manual, mechanical, or physical work), such that the output or result cannot be standardized in relation to a given period of time. Examples of individuals engaged in artistic professions include composers, novelists, actors, and musicians.

What Are Executives, Administrative
Employees, and Professionals Exempt From?

Each of the white-collar exemptions exempts qualifying employees from relevant sections of the Wage Orders (outside Salespersons are entirely exempt, however). More precisely, the Wage Orders' provisions governing hours and days of work, minimum wages, meal and rest periods, and overtime do not apply to employees who properly fall under the white-collar exemptions.

Other than the sections just specified, the remainder of the Wage Orders' provisions governing employee working conditions *do* apply to exempt employees. For example, the requirements that employers provide suitable seating for employees and maintain specific temperatures in the work environment still apply to exempt employees. These topics and other basic wage, hour, and working condition considerations are considered in more detail in the next section of this chapter.

Minimum Wage for Nonexempt Employees in California

As under federal law, all time in which an employee is suffered or permitted to work (that is, all time when an employer either requires or allows an employee to perform work) must be compensated under California law. Effective July 2009 and continued into 2013, the federal minimum wage rate has remained at $7.25 per hour. California employers must adhere to the current state (or local—for example, San Francisco or San Jose—if applicable; see textbox) minimum wage requirements.

In 2014, the minimum wage under California law will start at $8.00 per hour, a rate which has been in place since January 2008, but will change by mid-year. In September 2013, Governor Jerry Brown signed into law a bill that will raise California's minimum wage to $10 per hour by the year 2016. The state minimum wage will increase to $9.00 per hour effective July 1, 2014, and then increase again to $10.00 per hour effective January 1, 2016. Commensurate with these increases, the minimum compensation required for exempt employees whose wages are calculated based on the state minimum wage (that is, inside salespersons and employees who qualify for one of the white-collar exemptions) will also rise.

"Averaging" of Hours Not Permitted

Federal law under the FLSA allows an employer to average an employee's total weekly wages across "all hours" worked to see whether the FLSA minimum wage requirement is met. What does this mean? As an example, consider a nonexempt employee who regularly drives to a fixed location in San Diego to start his workday. The employee works from 9:30 a.m. to 5:00 p.m., with a 30-minute, unpaid, duty-free meal period each day. He is compensated at a rate of $350 per 35-hour workweek, so his regular rate is $10 per hour. Let's say that on a given day this employee attends a mandatory training at an off-site location. His employer requires that he and his co-workers take a company-provided shuttle from his regular worksite to the training and back. The shuttle leaves promptly at 9:30 a.m., and the planned return time is 5:00 p.m., when the employee would usually conclude his workday. As it happens, however, traffic is horrendous on the re-

Minimum Wage Ordinance Examples

San Francisco

The minimum wage rate for work performed in the city and county of San Francisco is set by local ordinance. The city's local rate—which exceeds both state and federal requirements—has increased annually since 2004. Effective January 1, 2013, the minimum wage for nonexempt employees working within the geographic boundaries of San Francisco is $10.55 per hour.

Employees covered by a bona fide collective bargaining agreement may be exempt from the requirements of the San Francisco Minimum Wage Ordinance, to the extent that such requirements are expressly waived in the collective bargaining agreement in clear and unambiguous terms.

San Jose

Effective January 1, 2014, the minimum wage rate for employees working in the city of San Jose is $10.15 per hour. This rate will increase annually by the cost of living.

turn trip, and the employee does not arrive back to his usual site (that is, where his car is parked) until 6:00 p.m.

Under federal law, the employer could take the employee's total weekly wages ($350.00) and divide by the total hours actually worked that week (36, due to the extra hour of travel time coming back from the training) to get an average hourly rate of $9.72 per hour—well above even the state minimum wage requirement. However, such "averaging" is *not* allowed under California law, which requires that employees be paid at least minimum wage for "every hour" worked. Thus, with regard to the example above, the employer would be required to pay the employee at least minimum wage (that is, $8.00 under state law) for that extra hour of travel time, resulting in a total compensation of at least $358.00 for the week in question.

Other Wage Requirements for Nonexempt Employees

Reporting to Work Pay

If an employee reports to work at his or her regularly scheduled time, but the employer finds it necessary to send that person home because there is no work, the Wage Orders require that the employee must be paid for reporting to work, even if no work is performed. Specifically, an employee must be paid for at least one-half his or her scheduled hours, but in no event less than two or more than four hours. If the employee is required to report to work a second time during the same day, he or she must receive at least two additional hours of work or pay for the second appearance.

Be aware that these provisions do not apply when work is interrupted by natural disasters or other causes outside the employer's control; when operations cannot begin due to a threat to company property or employees, or when recommended by civil authorities; or if public utilities are not operating. They also do not apply for individuals regularly scheduled to work less than two hours or for individuals on paid "standby."

Overtime Requirements for Nonexempt Employees

The FLSA measures overtime in terms of hours worked in a week. Federal law simply requires that nonexempt employees be paid one and one-half times their "regular rate" for all hours worked over 40 in a workweek, regardless of how many of these hours are worked in any one day.

In California, however, the Eight-Hour-Day Restoration and Workplace Flexibility Act of 1999 and the 2000 Wage Order amendments reestablished an eight-hour workday in California. Doing so has created significant differences between California and federal methods for how employees earn overtime. As a result, nonexempt California employees earn both daily and weekly overtime.

Daily Overtime

Nonexempt employees working in California must be paid at least one and one-half times ("time and a half") their regular rate of pay for hours worked over eight in a workday and two times ("double time") their regular rate for hours worked over 12 in a workday.

Weekly Overtime

In addition to any daily overtime earned, nonexempt employees must be paid at least time and a half for hours worked over 40 in a workweek. California employees are not entitled to receive overtime twice for the same hours, so weekly overtime does not apply if the employee has already received daily overtime for any hours worked over 40 in the workweek.

Alternative Workweek Schedule (AWS)

California's daily overtime requirements may seem particularly onerous for employers whose business needs require that employees work shifts of more than eight hours per workday. Such employers should not abandon *all* hope, however. California Labor Code 511, as well as many of the Wage Orders, provides that an employer may establish an alternative workweek schedule (AWS). The Code defines an AWS as "any regularly scheduled workweek requiring an employee to work more than eight hours in a 24-hour period." Effectively, under an AWS employees may agree that they will be paid at regular "straight" time for hours that would usually be considered "daily overtime" under the default statutory provisions.

Thus, a company operating in California could schedule employees for a regular 4/10 schedule (that is, four 10-hour workdays comprising a 40-hour workweek) without being subject to claims for daily overtime pay under state law. *However*—and this point must be emphasized—the procedure for putting such an arrangement in place is laid out with detailed specificity in the Wage Orders. Employers that fail to follow this procedure *exactly* as it is written may face steep penalties.

Employees may express a preference for the alternative workweek schedule because they could enjoy having to work fewer days in a week. However, establishing an AWS that will withstand the scrutiny of the DLSE is not simply a matter of employees' agreeing to work more hours per shift without demanding daily overtime. Employers must fulfill various requirements relating to notice, timing, and paperwork. A secret ballot election must be conducted following a specific protocol. An AWS that is not established in *strict accordance* with state requirements will be found invalid under state law, thereby exposing an employer to significant liability for unpaid overtime and statutory penalties.

So, if you're tempted to try an AWS, do it right the first time—with the assistance of experienced legal counsel.

Day of Rest Requirements

Aside from overtime, federal law says little about employee work hours or scheduling. Under California law, however, employees are entitled to one day's rest in seven in a given workweek. There are some exceptions to this rule (that is, in emergencies, in agriculture, or under a collective bargaining agreement), but even in these cases a premium must be paid.

Pursuant to the Wage Orders, nonexempt employees in California must be paid at least time and a half for the first eight hours worked on the seventh consecutive day of work in any single workweek. For hours worked over eight on the seventh day, nonexempt employees are entitled to be paid at double time.

Break Requirements for Nonexempt Employees

Meal Breaks

One of the most significant departures from federal law under the California wage and hour scheme is the requirement for meal and rest breaks. When meal periods are given to employees, to be considered "unpaid" under federal law the meal must be at least 30 minutes long, and the employee must be uninterrupted and completely relieved of all work duties during the meal break.

California *requires* employers to provide a duty-free, uninterrupted meal period of at least 30 minutes to employees during the first five hours of work. Employees who work over 10 hours/day must be provided a second duty-free meal period of at least 30 minutes.

Unless a valid waiver has been executed by the employee (see the next section), the employee *must* be relieved of all job duties ("off duty") during the statutory meal period. Additionally, if the employee is not free to leave the employer's premises, the meal period is considered "on duty." This means not only that the employee must be compensated for the on-duty meal period but that the employer must also pay a statutory penalty to the employee.

By comparison, the FLSA has no meal period requirement and therefore does not prohibit employers from requiring employees to stay on the premises during their meal period. This distinction is important for health care employers because Wage Orders 4-2001 and 5-2001 apply the FLSA "hours worked" definition to employees in the "health care industries." As such in California, hospital employees can be required to remain on the hospital's premises while taking their duty-free meal period.

State law further requires that employees record their time (punch in and punch out) when taking their meal period.

Given the complexity of the meal period requirements and recent indications that meal period policies are becoming a "hot" issue for plaintiffs' attorneys, employers should take steps to ensure that any written policy regarding meal periods for their California employees accurately and *fully* summarizes the law in this area, including by informing employees that (a) they are entitled to receive a first meal period when they work more than five hours and a second meal period when they work more than 10 hours; (b) meal periods must be provided by no later than the 5th and 10th hours of work; and (c) the meal period must be duty-free, uninterrupted, unimpeded, and not discouraged. See Table 1.3.

Table 1.3. Summary of Meal Period Requirements

Shift Duration In Hours	0 Meal Breaks	1 Meal Break Due	2 Meal Breaks Due
0-3 hours of actual work	X		
3-6 hours of actual work		unless valid waiver	
6-10 hours of actual work		meal period to be taken before beginning of 5th hour of work	
10-12 hours of actual work			• unless valid waiver of second break • first meal period to be taken before beginning of 5th hour of work
12-18 hours of actual work			• no waiver of either break available • first meal period taken before beginning of 5th hour of work • second meal break to be taken by end of 12th hour of work

Meal Period Waiver

Employees who work up to six hours/day may waive a meal period by mutual agreement with their employer. Additionally, employees who work between 10 and 12 hours in a workday may waive the second meal period with the mutual consent of their employer, provided that they have not waived their first meal period.

In both cases, the employer must secure a written waiver signed by the employee. The waiver must explicitly indicate that the employee can revoke it at will and without notice.

Rest Breaks

Again, employers are not obligated to provide employees with meal or rest periods under federal law. In contrast, California law *requires* employers to provide a paid rest period of at least 10 consecutive minutes for every four hours worked (or major fraction thereof). See Table 1.4.

Table 1.4. Summary of Rest Period Requirements	
Hours of Work	**Rest Periods Required**
0-3.5	0
3.5-6.0	1
6.0-10.0	2
10.0-14.0	3
14.0-18.0	4

"Provide" means the employer must make such breaks available to employees, but need not ensure that employees take them; employees are free to forego a rest period if they so choose. A rest period is not required for employees whose total daily work time is less than three and one-half hours.

Rest periods should be taken in the middle of each work period as much as possible. For example, an employee who is scheduled from 8:00 a.m. to 5:00 p.m. should be given midmorning and midafternoon rest periods.

A Note Regarding Breast-Feeding Breaks (Lactation Accommodation)

Under federal law, employers must provide reasonable break time for an employee to express breast milk for her nursing child for one year after the child's birth whenever the employee has need to express milk. The break time need not be paid. The employer must provide a place (not a bathroom) for the employee to express breast milk.

State law provides that all employees who are nursing mothers may take breaks as needed for the purpose of breast-feeding or expressing breast milk. An employee may use her regularly scheduled meal break and/or paid rest breaks for this purpose and, if necessary, may take additional unpaid breaks each time she needs to breast-feed or to express milk (to maintain supply and comfort).

California employees who wish to take such breaks should give their employer advance notice so that schedules can be adjusted to meet business needs. The employer must make a private room available to all nursing mothers for such breaks.

Other Working Conditions Established by the Wage Orders

California's Wage Orders place other requirements on businesses, totally outside anything found in the FLSA. The two biggest that have already led to significant litigation involve suitable seating and maintaining a reasonable temperature in the work environment.

Seating Requirements

The Wage Orders require that "suitable seats" must be provided for all working employees when the nature of their work reasonably permits the use of seats. In addition, an adequate number of suitable seats must be placed near the work area of employees whose work requires them to stand, so that employees may use the seats when they are not engaged in active duties.

Although the seating requirements have been a part of the Wage Orders for many years, they have recently received increased attention from plaintiffs' attorneys, particularly in the retail industry.

In contrast, there is no equivalent federal requirement that employers provide seating to employees.

Indoor/Outdoor Temperature Requirements

The Wage Orders further specify certain requirements relating to the work atmosphere—literally. That is, work areas must be maintained at a temperature that provides "reasonable comfort consistent with industry-wide standards" for the work being performed. The Orders specify that employee bathrooms must be kept at a temperature of at least 68 degrees. Employers are also required to take steps to reduce excess humidity in the workplace. However, the temperature provisions of the Wage Orders allow that to the extent any provision conflicts with federal or state energy guidelines, the energy guidelines should prevail.

Though many claims relating to excessive indoor and outdoor temperatures in the work environment have been brought by the California Division of Occupational Safety and Health (Cal/OSHA), private claims alleging a violation of the specific temperature requirements set forth in the Wage Orders being brought by the Labor Commissioner's Office seem to be hard to find. Nor does it seem that any lawsuits have been filed pursuant to the California Private Attorneys General Act as the agent for the state labor law enforcement agencies with regard to this issue. Of course, this does not mean that some plaintiffs' counsel will not attempt to bring such a suit—indeed, prior to the recent flood of cases alleging violation of the similar Wage Order provisions relating to seating, the labor commissioner had not appeared to have brought any "seats" claims, either.

2

California Wage
and Hour Law, Part II:
Statutory Requirements and
the Risk of Noncompliance

In Chapter 1, the focus was on a discussion of California's unique wage and hour regulatory scheme, specifically on the basics of the Industrial Welfare Commission (IWC) Wage Orders and how they imposed individualized requirements on the different industries found in the state. At this point, you may wonder what else there is to discuss. Well, the short answer is, a lot. The long answer to that question is the subject of this chapter, where we'll discuss the California Labor Code, or CLC. The CLC works in conjunction with, and often relies on, an understanding of the IWC Wage Orders (which is why it was important to cover those first).

In carrying on the theme of a business moving into California, this chapter covers the employment relationship from the obligations placed on a company at its start all the way though to what is required at the (hopefully not too bitter) end. Imagine you have been given the honor (or burden) to move to California to open up your company's first west coast facility. What are the challenges you'll face? And how do they differ from employing workers anywhere else in the country?

Defining the Employment Relationship

Fundamental to grasping how California wage and hour law differs from federal law (and from the law of other states) is a clear understanding of what is meant by "employment relationship." This is a critical initial consideration because the existence of an employment relationship is a precursor to almost all California wage and hour law application. Though not even California's unique wage and hour scheme applies when there is no employment relationship, it is possible for such a relationship to be found even when the employer does not intend to create one.

The IWC Wage Orders define "employ" as "to engage, suffer, or permit to work." An employer is anyone who "directly or indirectly, or through an agent or any other person, employs or exercises control over the wages, hours or working conditions of any person" ("person" in this context can be an individual, association, partnership, corporation, and so on). And finally, "employee" means "any person employed by an employer."

Let's put that all together. An employment relationship amounts to a relationship in which a person or business of some sort engages, suffers, or permits a person to work, while exercising control over that person's wages, hours, and working conditions.

But wait, you say . . . an independent contractor might meet that definition. Well, not exactly—but that certainly raises a good point. California's wage and hour protections do *not* apply to independent contractor relationships, and as such the distinction is vital to know—particularly because of the risks involved in misclassifying someone as a contractor when he or she is, in reality, an employee. Such misclassifications give rise to significant risk of liability, so employers should base employee classification on a thorough analysis of all the relevant factors.

Distinguishing "Employees" from "Independent Contractors": The Right to Control

The right to control is perhaps the most important factor—and that which California courts look to first—in distinguishing between an employee and independent contractor. According to the California Supreme Court, the "right to control" refers to an employer's right to direct and control the manner and means of performing work. Where the right to direct and control is found, the worker is deemed an employee.

Yet, the right to control is not determinative. Its absence does not mean the worker is *not* an employee—in this situation California courts have looked to other, secondary factors. Some questions employers should ask themselves (that courts have found persuasive) include:

- Can the working relationship be terminated at will/without cause?
- Is payment made to the individual by job or by some unit of time?
- Does the employer supply the necessary equipment, tools, and/or place of work?
- Is the work being performed by the individual part of the employer's regular business?

These are just a few of several factors that courts have considered, and they are important questions to keep in mind. After all, misclassification remains a hot topic for plaintiffs' lawyers, with the potential result that an employer may be required to pay out large sums to compensate misclassified employees for such things as unpaid overtime, missed meal and rest periods, and penalties for any other wage and hour violations they did not even know applied to these employees. For example, in the case of *Labrie v. UPS Supply Chain Solutions, Inc.* (2009), delivery drivers of a nationwide delivery service brought an action under both California and federal law against their employer alleging they were misclassified as independent contractors. The drivers sought consequent unpaid overtime and associated California penalties. After the class of 380 drivers was certified, the employer settled for $12.8 million, with two-thirds of the recovery going to the California drivers alone.

What about Federal Law?

Compare the California definition of employment relationship above with the rules under federal law. Federal law applies the "economic realities" test to define the employment relationship. Though the name is different, the factors considered are quite similar, primary of which is the employer's right to control the employee's work and the manner or means of performing the work. Other factors include whether the person performing the work provides his or her own tools and equipment or has incurred a substantial cost (for example, hired his or her own labor) or even if that person has the opportunity to profit from his or her management skill while performing the job. These factors each weigh in favor of the person being an independent contractor. Factors weighing in favor of an employment relationship are whether the relationship is permanent or indefinite and whether the person is performing a service that is part of the employer's regular business or is working in an ancillary capacity.

Joint Employer Liability

Now that we've established what it takes to have an employment relationship, it bears mention that an employee can actually have more than one employer for purposes of assigning liability under California's wage laws. In other words, two (or possibly more) distinct employers may be held jointly and severally liable for compliance with all applicable wage and hour provisions relating to a single employee. This situation commonly arises when employers seek temporary help from staffing agencies, as temp workers from a staffing agency may be considered joint employees of both the business they are placed at and the agency that placed them.

When two employers are found to be entirely independent and disassociated from each other, there will be no joint liability. When, however, both employers benefit from the employee's work or the employee actually performs work for each employer during the week, the employers will be considered joint employers for liability purposes if any one of the following occurs:

- There is an arrangement between the employers to share the employee's services.
- One employer is acting directly or indirectly in the interest of the other employer.
- The employers are found to directly or indirectly share control of the employee because one employer controls the other employer.

Joint employment can have both benefits and drawbacks. The most significant drawback is potential shared liability for failure to comply with wage and hour requirements, including minimum wage and overtime pay, as well as other statutory requirements. Also important (and sometimes overlooked) is the fact that all hours worked by a joint employee for his or her joint employers must be aggregated to determine the number of hours an employee has worked, for purposes of overtime calculation and other hours-dependent considerations.

On the plus side, joint employers can each take credit for all payment made to the employee by the other joint employer(s) in determining compliance with minimum wage and overtime pay requirements. Of course, such a "benefit" would be cold comfort at best when an employer does not intend to create any employment relationship in the first place. To guard against unwanted (and unanticipated) potential liability, employers should therefore seek legal counsel when entering into contracts for the performance of services by temporary workers, or with specialized companies that contract to provide housekeeping, maintenance, food and beverage, or other discrete services at an employer's facility.

The Beginning of the Employment Relationship

So, with that additional foundational discussion out of the way, we can move on to the practical concerns of most employers—how to actually *employ* people legally in California. The most effective way to cover this topic is to look at it from the perspective of a company moving into California for the first time. Let's assume that the company is a very successful one and covers many states across the country but has always avoided the Golden State before now. Let's go one step further and assume that *you* are transferred to the new California location from outside the state and told to get the business up and running from a staffing standpoint. With that goal in mind, where does such a relationship begin?

We Hired Our First Employees. What Do We Do Now?

California wage and hour laws govern the employment relationship from the moment of hire, before an employee has even performed any work for the company. Therefore, compliance with the law is essential from the very first instance of operations.

Providing Notice-of-Pay Information on Hire

Under California law, new hires must receive written notice of certain pay-related information. This requirement is unique to California— federal law does not have an equivalent requirement, other than the requirement that employers post the U.S. Department of Labor (DOL) minimum wage and overtime poster in a conspicuous location for employees to see.

California specifically requires that employees be informed in writing of the following information at the time of hire:

1. Pay rate and basis for the pay rate (for example, salary, commission, hourly).
2. Any allowances (*if* any are claimed as part of the minimum wage, including meal and lodging allowances).
3. Regular payday.
4. Employer's name (including any "doing business as" names used by the employer).
5. Physical address of the employer's main or principal place of business, and a mailing address (if different).
6. Employer's telephone number.
7. Name, address, and telephone number of the employer's workers' compensation insurance carrier.
8. Any other information the Labor Commissioner's Office deems material and important.

This final "catch-all" requirement should not scare you. It should instead make you aware that these requirements can be supplemented as the labor commissioner deems necessary, and as such, new requirements can and will arise from time to time. However, if you've provided the information listed in items 1-7 above, you have more likely than not satisfied your initial burden.

Establishing Working Hours

Well, OK, step one is done. You have employees. Now what? Now that you hired some folks, notified them when and how much they will be paid, and given them a whole range of other important information, you need to get them scheduled to work. The first step in this process is to decide what constitutes a workday and a workweek for the business. How a California employer defines these key wage and hour terms plays a crucial role in determining how—and how much—it must pay employees for daily and weekly overtime under state law.

Defining the "Workday" or "Day"

Section 500 of the California Labor Code defines "workday" or "day" as "any consecutive 24-hour period commencing at the same time each calendar day." This definition allows employers room to define their workday to best suit their business needs. As long as the workday begins at the same time every day, it can begin at whatever time the employer chooses. If an employer does not define a specific workday, the California Division of Labor Standards Enforcement (DLSE) will automatically treat the workday as beginning at midnight.

Defining the "Workweek" or "Week"

Section 500 also defines "workweek" or "week" is as "any seven consecutive days, starting with the same calendar day each week." A workweek is a fixed and recurring set of seven consecutive "workdays." An employer can define its workweek to meet its business needs, as long as it begins on the same workday each week and continues for seven consecutive days. If the employer does not define a specific workweek, the DLSE will treat the workweek as midnight to midnight, Sunday to Saturday.

Split Shift Requirements

Wage Order Number 4 defines a split shift as "a work schedule, which is interrupted by non-paid non-working periods established by the employer, other than bona fide rest or meal periods."

An additional hour's pay at state minimum wage (as of January 1, 2008, $8 per hour until the next scheduled increase on July 1, 2014) must be paid as a premium to employees who work a split shift only if the employee's total earnings for that day are not at least $8 more than their hours worked times minimum wage.

Split Shifts: An Example

An employee earns $9/hour. She works a seven-hour split shift, from 8:00 a.m. to noon and then from 6:00 p.m. to 9:00 p.m. She is paid $63 for her shift (7 hours × $9/hour = $63). Is her employer in compliance with state law?

No. Assuming a state minimum wage of $8 per hour, the employer is required to pay the split shift worker at least $64 in this example (7-hour shift × $8 minimum hourly wage, plus an additional hour of pay at the $8 minimum wage rate = $64).

Another way to think of this rule is, an employee who works a split shift must receive compensation equal to or greater than minimum wage times the number of hours worked plus 1.

Under federal law, split shift premiums must be included in the regular rate of pay for purposes of calculating overtime.

Call-In Pay Requirements

Good news: There is no specific federal law regarding call-in pay. Bad news: There *is* a specific California law about it. A California employee who is called in to work on a day for which he or she is not scheduled *must* be paid for at least two hours, even if the employee in fact works less than two hours that day. Many companies run into problems with this when calling off-duty employees "for just one thing." In California, a 10-minute off-duty call can equal two hours of pay.

On-Call Guidelines

When nonexempt employees work on an "on-call" basis, a California employer must be sensitive to whether such time spent on call is compensable. The following guidelines apply when nonexempt employees work on an on-call basis:

- If the employee is required to remain on the employer's premises during on-call time, all such time must be paid.
- If the employee is not required to remain on the employer's premises when on call, but is required to carry a beeper or cellphone, whether this time is paid on-call time depends on how much freedom the employee has to pursue his or her own

pursuits. If the expectation that the employee respond to such calls within a certain amount of time so restricts the employee that he or she cannot pursue personal activities while on call, the entire amount of time the employee spends on call should be considered compensable time.

- Should an individual be contacted when on call, the time that person spends on the telephone or at a work location performing job responsibilities must be paid. As a general rule, travel time to return to the worksite is not compensable unless the employee's entire on-call shift is considered paid time as described above.
- An employer must also take into consideration how frequently the employee is contacted during on-call time, even if the employee does nothing more than respond to the phone call. If an employer is calling or paging an employee so often that the employee's freedom of activity is limited, the entire time that individual spends on call may be compensable.
- If it is determined that on-call time is paid time, overtime should be paid according to state and federal guidelines.

Contrast this multilayered analysis with that of the federal rules, which state that on-call time is compensable only if the employee's personal freedom is so restricted that the employee is effectively on duty.

Paying Your Employees in California

Establishing a Payday for Nonexempt Employees

Federal law leaves it to the states to dictate the timing of wage payments. California takes that obligation and runs away with it. In California, an employer must establish a regular payday and post a notice that shows the day, time, and location of payment. Additionally, wages for most employees must be paid at least twice in each calendar month, on the days the employer has designated as regular paydays. Further, wages earned between the 1st and 15th days, inclusive, of any calendar month must be paid before the 26th day of that month. Wages earned between the 16th and the last day of the month must be paid by the 10th day of the next month. Failure to pay within the allotted time can mean huge penalties for the company.

The case of *Hasty v. Electronic Arts* (2006) is one illustrative $14.9 million example. In *Hasty*, a computer-gaming company settled a class action brought by two plaintiffs on behalf of 600 programmers. The plaintiffs alleged, in part, that they were not paid twice during each calendar month. These allegations stemmed from the company's allegedly misclassifying the programmers as "exempt." This example also underscores how one failure can result in derivative violations, yielding big paydays for employees.

Payment of Exempt Employees

Executive, administrative, and professional employees can be paid once a month, on or before the 26th day of the month, if employees are paid the entire month's salary, including the "unearned" portion between payday and the end of the month. If an employer chooses to, it can pay these employees more frequently.

Method of Pay (Paying Wages by Direct Deposit)

Payment by direct deposit is voluntary in California. An employer may deposit wages in an employee's bank account, provided the employee voluntarily authorizes the deposit to a financial institution of his or her choice with a place of business in the state. There is no specific federal law addressing electronic pay practices.

Wage Statements

One of the hottest areas of class-action litigation in California involves employers' making what seem to be minor technical mistakes or omissions on wage statements. The problem isn't the pay itself but the *statement* that goes along with the payment.

California Labor Code Section 226 requires that employers give employees wage statements that include nine categories of information:

- Gross wages earned.
- Total hours worked (except for salaried exempt employees).
- Number of piece-rate units and rate per unit (if paid by piece rate).
- All deductions (employee-requested deductions may be aggregated).
- Net wages earned.

- Dates of pay period (both beginning and ending dates).
- Employee name and last four digits of the employee's Social Security number or company ID number.
- Name and address of "legal entity" that is the employer.
- All applicable hourly rates in effect during the pay period *and* corresponding number of hours worked at each hourly rate.

The CLC provides for statutory penalties of $50 per employee for the initial pay period in which a violation occurs and $100 per employee per pay period thereafter, up to a maximum of $4,000. Alleged failure to comply with wage statement requirements has become an increasingly common claim in class-action lawsuits under California law, so it is important for employers to ensure that pay stubs contain all of the necessary information. Seven-figure settlements are not uncommon for companies that fail to comply with all nine requirements— including some violations that might seem innocent such as omitting the legal entity name or the employee's ID or Social Security number.

Commission Earnings

What about Employees Who Receive Earned Commissions?

State law defines "commission" as compensation paid to any person in connection with the sale of the employer's property or services and based proportionately on the value thereof. A commission does not include short-term productivity bonuses such as those paid to retail clerks. It also does not include bonus and profit-sharing plans, unless the employer has offered to pay a fixed percentage of sales or profits as compensation for work to be performed.

Commissions are not considered earned until they are reasonably calculable. Sales employees in California must be paid commission earnings, if due, as soon as all the information necessary to calculate them is available, and in no event later than the next regularly scheduled payday.

Written Commission Contracts

Effective January 1, 2013, California started requiring all employers contemplating payment in commissions to put the agreement in writing and to identify the method by which the commissions will be computed and paid. Employers must give a copy of the agreement to every employee who is a party to it, and must retain a signed receipt of the contract from each employee.

California law also provides that when a commission agreement expires and the parties continue to work under the expired agreement's terms, the contract terms are presumed to remain in full force and effect until the agreement is superseded or either party terminates the employment.

The new law applies to all employers with commissioned employees in California, whether or not the employer is located in California.

In contrast to state law, there is no federal law requiring written commission agreements.

Note on Commission and Piece-Rate Pay Plans— Employers Beware!

As discussed in Chapter 1, California law requires that employees be paid at least minimum wage for *each* hour worked. Perhaps not surprisingly, courts have recently interpreted this to mean that commission and piece-rate pay plans violate the law if they do not *separately* pay employees at least minimum wage for each hour of work not directly related to earning a commission (that is, selling) or to earning a "piece." This interpretation puts many commission or piece-rate plans squarely in the crosshairs if employers do not separately pay employees for such work activities as attending meetings, pre- and post-piece or commission work, and mandatory rest periods. Plans that do not pay employees a base or nonrecoverable draw of at least minimum wage for each hour worked, and then commissions or piece rates in addition to that base pay, could violate the law.

The consequences of these recent developments are far reaching because they apply to all nonexempt employees who are paid under a commission or piece-rate plan and all exempt employees who remain subject to minimum wage requirements under the commission sales exemption, regardless of the amount of income the employee may receive under the plan itself. It is recommended that employers examine existing piece-rate and commission plans and contact employment counsel to address any concerns. This area is still evolving, and practitioners and employers are paying close attention—with good reason.

Gratuities, Tips, and Tip Pooling

In the event you want to open a business in which employees routinely receive tips, there are special rules here, too. "Gratuity" is defined under California law as a tip, gratuity, or money paid, given to, or left for an employee by a patron of a business that is over and above the actual amount due for services rendered or for goods, food, drink, or articles sold or served to patrons.

Federal law defines "tips" as a sum presented by a customer as a gift or gratuity in recognition of some service performed for him or her. Tips must be paid in cash or a cash equivalent and include amounts transferred by the employer to the employee pursuant to credit card receipts that include tips.

California law prohibits employers and their agents from sharing in or keeping any portion of an employee's tips. It is illegal for employers to make wage deductions from an employee's tips or to use such tips as direct or indirect credits against an employee's earned wages. This means that in California, unlike under federal law, there is no lower or alternative minimum wage for "tipped employees." The law states that tips are the sole property of the employee or employees to whom they are given. Furthermore, tips paid by credit card must be given to employees by the next regular payday following the date the person giving the tip authorized the credit card payment. This is a huge departure from federal law and can catch the unwary employer off guard.

Tip Pooling under State Law

State law permits involuntary "tip pooling" in California. Thus, employers may require that an employee share his or her tips with other staff members who provide service in a restaurant setting. If an employer chooses to require tip pooling, tips should be distributed among the employees who provide "direct table service." This category includes servers, bussers, bartenders, and hosts/hostesses, but *not* supervisors or managers even if direct service to customers is provided. California courts have recently expanded this group to include anyone in the "chain of service," but not the employer itself.

Vacation Time Accrual: No "Use It or Lose It" Policies Here

In California, vacation and paid time off (PTO) are considered a form of wages that an employee earns, or accrues, as he or she works. These benefits are considered vested as they are earned and part of the employment contract.

How Are Vacation and PTO Different?

Vacation refers to any paid time off earned as a benefit of working and includes so-called floating holidays not associated with any particular date. Employees use their accrued vacation time to "pay" for personal time away from work, for whatever reason they choose. By comparison, PTO may lump together vacation, sick leave, holidays, floating holidays, and any other variation on the theme of "paid time off." In California, PTO is treated as vacation and likewise vests when accrued.

Whether vacation time or PTO, once accrued, both vest; an employer cannot take earned time away if the employee does not use it, which is known as a "use it or lose it" policy. Such policies are not allowed in California, although an employer that chooses to offer vacation or PTO time may set a "cap" on the maximum amount of such time an employee may accrue.

An employee must be paid upon termination for any vested and unused vacation or PTO at the same wage rate the employee was earning at the time of termination.

What about Sick Leave?

Under California law, sick leave—that is, time off that can only be used for specified purposes such as medical treatment, recovery from illness, and caring for a sick family member—does *not* vest like PTO or vacation and can be forfeited if not used by a certain time. Because employers are generally not required by law to offer sick leave, the employer's policy will control (unless the employer has employees working in San Francisco, as noted in the textbox below). Therefore, an employer's sick leave policy should be carefully crafted to outline accrual rate and forfeiture, use restrictions, and any requirements that must be fulfilled before use (for example, specific notice requirements).

Holiday Pay

Holiday pay, as such, is not required in California. An employer that chooses to offer paid or unpaid time off for holidays can choose which holidays to observe and the eligibility requirements to receive such pay. This gives employers significant flexibility in crafting a holiday pay policy as they wish—for example, requiring that employees work

San Francisco Sick Leave Policy

The city and county of San Francisco have a mandatory sick leave policy that applies to all employees working there. Under the policy, employers must provide one hour of paid sick leave for every 30 hours an employee works (1.33 hours per 40-hour workweek). This is capped at 72 hours if the employer has 10 or more employees, including part-time or temporary employees, or 40 hours if the employer has fewer than 10. These hours can carry over from year to year, subject to the applicable cap, but do not need to be paid out on termination.

The requirement kicks in after 90 days of employment. An employee can use his or her sick leave hours for personal illnesses or to care for a sick child, parent, sibling, grandparent, grandchild, or registered domestic partner. If the employee has no spouse or domestic partner, he or she may designate someone whom he or she can use these hours to care for. This designation must occur within 10 days of hire and can be changed annually.

Note: The San Francisco Sick Leave Ordinance sets a *minimum* requirement. An employer does not have to provide additional sick leave if its existing policy meets or exceeds the San Francisco Sick Leave Ordinance's requirements.

the day before or the day after the holiday to receive the holiday pay. Employers should clearly identify at the beginning of the year which holidays they will observe, whether they will be paid, and what will happen if an employee is required to work on a designated holiday.

Floating Holidays

Employers should be aware that under state law, floating holidays are considered to accrue and vest just as vacation time and PTO do. Reasonable caps on accrual are allowed, and an employer may require employees to use or cash out accrued floating holidays on an annual basis. As with vacation time, an employee must be paid immediately upon termination for any vested and unused floating holidays.

Other Pay Considerations for California Employees

OK, so now we have employees, schedules, pay, and time off figured out. Good—you are almost ready to actually start your new employees working. Just a few (OK, several) more things.

Calculating the Regular Rate of Pay

It may seem counterintuitive, but an employee's "regular rate" of pay for overtime pay purposes is not always the same as his or her normal rate. Instead, the regular rate reflects the employee's *actual* rate of pay, which includes hourly earnings as well as most other types of compensation, such as commissions and certain bonuses. When an employee earns commissions or bonuses, the regular rate must be calculated weekly to determine his or her overtime rate. Thus, it is important to know how and when to calculate the regular rate.

Regular Rate for Commission or Other Pay Incentive for Employees

To calculate the regular rate in which an employee's pay includes commissions, bonuses, or other types of compensation (for example, piece work earnings), an employer should divide total compensation for the week by the total number of hours worked. This will determine the regular rate for purposes of calculating the employee's overtime rate. The employee's overtime rate is equal to one and one half times his or her regular rate.

Weighted Average for Multiple Hourly Rates

Additionally, if the work is truly different, California employers can pay different rates for different or even nonproductive time, such as time spent traveling. To calculate an employee's regular rate when that employee receives multiple rates of pay, an employer needs to use the "weighted average" method. This method again requires dividing total compensation by total hours worked for that week. This amount yields the weighted average of the employee's regular rate. This rate divided by two yields the employee's overtime premium. Add this premium to the hourly rate for type of work the employee is performing when earning overtime at time and one-half. If double time is due, you will add the regular rate itself to the rate for the work being performed to calculate the employee's double-time rate for that work.

Regular Rate for Salaried, Nonexempt Employees

If the employee is salaried but not exempt, his or her weekly salary should be divided by the number of hours it is meant to cover, up to a maximum of 40 hours, to arrive at the employee's regular rate.

Weighted Averages: An Example

An employee earns $12.00 per hour for time spent working, and $10.00 per hour for travel time. In a given week, the employee works 40 hours and spends 10 hours traveling (for work-related purposes, of course). Having spent a total of 50 hours in work-related activities that week, it is safe to conclude the employee is due some weekly (or even daily) overtime. But at what rate?

40 hours @ $12.00 = $480.00 (total compensation for working time that week)
10 hours @ $10.00 = $100.00 (total compensation for travel time that week)

Total hours for the week = 50
Total compensation for the week = $580.00

Divide the total compensation by the total hours:
$580.00/50 = $11.60 (this is the employee's regular rate)

Divide the regular rate by 2 to get the overtime premium:
$11.60/2 = $5.80 (this is the employee's overtime premium)

The employee's overtime rate of pay will be equal to the wage rate for the activity performed during overtime, plus the overtime premium. So, to conclude our example:

If the employee is earning overtime while working, his overtime rate is $12.00 + $5.80 = $17.80.

If the employee is earning overtime while traveling, his overtime rate is $10.00 + $5.80 = $15.80.

Under the Fair Labor Standards Act (FLSA), if a salaried, nonexempt employee's salary is understood to compensate him or her for the hours worked that week, the actual hours can be used to determine the regular rate. In contrast, California prohibits the use of this "fluctuating workweek" method to calculate the regular rate for nonexempt, salaried employees. This means California overtime pay will typically be higher.

Rounding

No statute expressly authorizes rounding an employee's hours, but no statute specifically prohibits it, either. In practice rounding is allowed in California, as it is under federal law, when calculating the number of hours an employee has worked. For example, even the state

> ## Salaried, Nonexempt Employees: FLSA versus California
>
> *Consider a salaried, nonexempt employee earning $600 a week and working 60 hours in a particularly busy week.*
>
> Under the FLSA method, the employee's regular rate is $600/60 hours, or $10 per hour. The employee would be entitled to an additional $100 in overtime (1/2 x $10 x 20 hours).
>
> In California, the employee's regular rate is $600/40 hours, or $15 per hour. The employee is owed an extra $150 in overtime (1/2 x $15 x 20 hours).

labor commissioner rounds and will accept rounding to the nearest five minutes, or tenth or quarter of an hour, as long as doing so fairly compensates employees for all hours worked when extrapolated over a period of time.

Recent case law has also affirmed this practice, finding that employers may round employee time card entries to the nearest tenth of an hour as long as the practice is fair and neutral. The employer in this case prevailed by demonstrating that over time, its rounding practice did not result in a loss to the employee. Importantly, the employer also demonstrated that employees knew about its rounding policy. The court addressed rounding to only the nearest tenth of an hour, and did not approve rounding in larger increments such as to the nearest quarter of an hour. Understandably, if an employer rounds to larger fractions of an hour, there is more likely to be a long-term loss to the employee (and the practice is less likely to pass muster).

If an employer chooses to employ rounding as an administrative matter, it should make sure the policy is clear and understood by employees. Additionally, the labor commissioner instructs that employers should look to employees' actual work patterns to ascertain whether the time records with rounding taken into account accurately reflect those work patterns. As long as there is no routine underpayment and employees are clear that such a practice takes place, the employer's rounding policy will be acceptable.

Travel Time Compensation for Nonexempt Employees

California and federal law are mostly parallel in how they treat the compensability of travel time. However, in contrast to the requirement that employees must be compensated for the time they are "suffered or permitted to work," California law requires that employees be compensated for time spent "subject to the control" of the employer. This point of divergence can pose challenges for the employer, especially in the area of compensation for travel time.

The following are common scenarios that provide guidance as to whether travel time is compensable in California.

Same Day Travel

- Regular commute. Employee travel between home and work is generally not compensable under either California or federal law. However, if an employee is ever required to travel to a worksite other than the employee's regular worksite(s) (that is, for a special assignment, training or meeting location), the employer must compensate the employee's time spent traveling that exceeds the employee's normal commute time.

- "All in a day's work" travel. All travel time after the employee reports to work, such as travel from one work location to another during the workday, is compensable under both California and federal law. In addition, all travel time that is part of a day's work (such as travel back to the regular worksite after a morning meeting or travel from the regular worksite to an afternoon training) is paid time.

- "Special" commute. California requires all employees to be paid for time spent traveling to an out-of-town business meeting, training session, or any other event (including "errands" performed at the behest of the employer, such as making a stop on the way to or from the workplace to obtain or deliver an item for the employer). All travel time between home and a special assignment's location that exceeds an employee's normal commute time is considered compensable under California law.

Overnight Travel

All travel time during an employee's normal working hours between home and the out-of-town destination that exceeds the employee's normal commute time is compensable at the employee's regular rate of pay under both federal and California law. This includes travel from home to the airport or rail depot, etc. "Normal working hours" means the employee's regular schedule as applied to weekdays and weekends for purposes of determining compensability, even if the employee's normal working hours are Monday through Friday.

California and federal law differ on the compensability of travel time outside normal working hours. Under federal law, travel time outside an employee's normal working hours does not need to be compensated unless the employee is actually working while traveling. California makes no distinction between normal hours and outside normal hours—*all* travel time is compensable as time the employee is "subject to the control of the employer." Meal times and other times that the employee is free to engage in personal pursuits (for example, sleep time and time after "hotel arrival") are not compensable under either federal or California law.

For example, say a company requires all new employees to travel from their home state to the corporate headquarters in Chicago, Illinois, for two weeks of training at the start of the employment relationship. The employees' normal work schedule requires them to work from 8:00 a.m. to 5:00 p.m., Monday through Friday. If the company decided to have the trainees fly out between the hours of 8:00 a.m. and 5:00 p.m., under the FLSA it would be considered compensable work time *regardless* of what day the flight occurred. Outside of those regular work hours, however, such travel time would *not* be compensable under the FLSA, no matter how long the flight took.

In direct contrast to the federal rule, all of the California employees' travel time—irrespective of when it occurred—is fully compensable. Additionally, if the travel time occurred in the evening after the employees worked a full day, all the travel time would be compensable as overtime.

Note: Employers can set a separate hourly rate for employee travel time as long as it exceeds minimum wage. The employee must be informed of the different rate before he or she embarks on said travel.

Expenses for Required Uniforms

State law obligates an employer that requires its nonexempt employees to wear special uniforms (that is, uniforms that cannot reasonably be worn by an employee as regular clothing) to provide and maintain the uniforms, regardless of the employees' compensation.

Under federal law, it is unlawful for an employer to deduct the cost of a uniform or its maintenance from an employee's wages when the reduction reduces the wages of that employee below minimum wage. If wearing a clean uniform is required by law, by the employer, or by the nature of the work, the cost of renting or buying and maintaining the claim uniform may not be treated as wages for purposes of complying with minimum wage.

Deductions from Salary for Exempt Employees ("Docking")

To meet the salary basis test under California law, an employee must receive a predetermined amount that is not subject to reduction because of variations in the quality or quantity of the work performed for any week in which the employee performs work. Although exempt employees need not be paid for any workweek in which they perform no work, employers may not add or deduct from an exempt employee's salary on an hourly basis or daily basis except under very limited circumstances.

An employer's HR department should be involved in any decision to make a salary deduction to an exempt employee. Making an improper deduction may jeopardize the employee's exempt status.

Payment of Wages upon Separation from Employment

There is no federal law regarding payment of wages upon termination. The frequency within which wages must be paid and the time that wages must be paid upon termination is controlled by state law.

California law requires that an employer pay all earned wages—including all earned and unused vacation or PTO—to an employee immediately upon termination of the employment relationship, regardless of whether the termination is voluntary or involuntary, due to a reduction in the workforce or a result of the temporary nature of certain employment (for example, temporary/seasonal workers).

An employee who voluntarily resigns without prior notice must be paid all wages earned within 72 hours. Employees who provide at least 72 hours' notice of intent to quit must be paid at the time of separation.

No Deductions from Final Wages

Upon separation from employment, a California employer may *not* deduct any "bad debt" owed to the employer from an employee's wages unless such a deduction has been voluntarily authorized by the employee in writing.

Waiting Time Penalties

An employer that fails to pay final wages according to the above guidelines must pay an additional day of wages for each day the final wages are not paid, up to a total of 30 days. Therefore, if a company makes an error and shorts an employee as little as one hour of accrued vacation time, that employee is entitled to up to 30 days of *full* wages, plus the one hour.

Example

On February 1, an employee gives notice that she is resigning on February 14. The employee is owed all final wages on her last day of work, which is February 14. However, due to a clerical mistake her employer did not provide her with her final wages on February 14 and did not realize this error until February 18. In addition to her final wages (including accrued vacation time/PTO), the employee is now owed waiting time penalties for four days (the number of days her final wages were not available to her)

In one case brought by a one-day hair model against a large cosmetics company, the California Supreme Court weighed in on California's strong public policy favoring prompt wage payment. The company hired the model for $500 to model in a one-day show. She accepted, performed, and left—without getting paid. After going unpaid for two months, she sued for $15,000 in waiting time penalties and won, earning quite a paycheck for one day's work. This case underscores the importance of an employer's having a final paycheck both accurate and ready to go at the end of an employment relationship, whether by termination or some other conclusion. Any delays, however brief, can cause penalties to multiply, especially when a class of employees is involved.

California Record-Keeping Requirements

Records of Hours

California law requires employers to keep accurate records of hours worked by nonexempt employees. Such records must show employee's shift start and end times. Additionally, meal periods must be accurately recorded. The best practice is to have employees clock out and back in, or otherwise record their meal's start and end times. As mentioned previously, there are specific timing requirements for meal periods, which the time records should reflect. A recent California Supreme Court decision exemplified the importance of clocking in and out for meal periods, when one justice implied the failure to do so created a presumption that the employee was working during the meal break (that is, not properly relieved of all duty as required by the CLC). In essence, this practice combined with an appropriate policy prohibiting off-the-clock work can be extremely helpful to employers when faced with employee claims of missed meal periods

As usual, where there is a general rule under California wage and hour law, there are also specific exemptions. Specific industry or occupational Wage Orders, as well as certain CLC sections, allow for slight variations to the general hour-recording requirements. Employers should look to the Orders covering their industry or their employees for precise details.

Record Retention Guidelines

Under state law, an employer must maintain payroll information for a period of at least four years.

Note: These retention guidelines do not apply when a litigation hold is in effect. All documents subject to a litigation hold should be maintained as directed by the employer's risk management department and/or legal counsel.

Liability and the Private Attorneys General Act of 2004

As illustrated by select examples, an employer should expect that violations of state wage and hour requirements will carry consequences, often in the form of a statutory penalty on top of liability for unpaid compensation. There isn't sufficient space to detail all the statute-specific penalties in these chapters—such a subject could fill several books by itself. Nevertheless, this chapter cannot end without a discussion of the dreaded "PAGA."

The Labor Code Private Attorneys General Act of 2004 (PAGA) effectively deputized each employee of a California employer with the authority to sue individually or bring a class action to recover civil penalties for violations of the CLC. If a Labor Code provision does not provide a specific statutory penalty for a violation, the PAGA establishes a $100 penalty for the employer's first violation, and a $200 penalty for each additional violation, *per employee.*

Moreover, an employee bringing a PAGA claim on behalf of him or herself and other employees does not need to meet the same class-action prerequisites required for other claims. If this seems daunting, consider this: the PAGA *also* provides for recovery of attorney fees. There are plaintiffs' lawyers who do quite well for themselves in the Golden State, simply by representing individuals who bring successful claims under the PAGA. For all these reasons, employers should tread lightly and carry an accurate compass when operating in the murky waters of California wage and hour law.

Why California Employers Should Be Concerned about PAGA Penalties

A simple example demonstrates how PAGA penalties can multiply:

If an employer with 100 employees leaves off a single one of the categories of wage statement information that is required by law, *one time*, that employer potentially faces $10,000 in penalties (100 employees x $100 per violation = $10,000).

If the employer does it *twice*—fails to include that single category of information on the wage statement two pay periods in a row, for example—the employer now faces a total of $30,000 in penalties (100 employees x $200 per violation = $20,000, plus the $10,000 for the initial violation).

Yes, every violation after the first is penalized *doubly* under the PAGA (again, that penalty is *per violation* and *per employee*). You can imagine how the PAGA's penalty scheme can blossom into something particularly attractive to disgruntled employees seeking to bring a cause of action against their employer.

3

California Anti-Discrimination Laws:

Federal Law on Steroids

We've now covered, in Chapters 1 and 2, how to legally employ workers, pay them, and make sure their paychecks say all the right things. It's smooth sailing from here on out, right? Well, not quite.

Although compliance with wage and hour laws is critical, there are still a host of other laws and regulations that California imposes on companies that employ staff within the state. Next on the list of "laws to be aware of when doing business in California" are the state's aggressive anti-discrimination and anti-harassment laws.

Most businesses, and certainly those large enough to have a dedicated human resource department, are familiar with the myriad federal anti-discrimination laws—the Civil Rights Act of 1964 (Title VII), the Americans with Disabilities Act (ADA), the Age Discrimination in Employment Act (ADEA), and the Genetic Information Nondiscrimination Act (GINA). By now it should come as no surprise that California takes these federal laws and enhances, expands, and (in some cases) overrides the federal laws through its own statutory scheme.

In many states, the U.S. Equal Employment Opportunity Commission (EEOC) enforces the federal anti-discrimination laws with passion. In California, however, the EEOC is often an afterthought, hanging around in the background while disgruntled employees, aggressive plaintiff's attorneys, and the state Department of Fair Employment and Housing (DFEH) pursue relief under the far more expansive scope of California's anti-discrimination legislation—including (among others) the Fair Employment and Housing Act (FEHA), the Unruh Civil Rights Act (Unruh), and the California Equal Pay Act.

In this chapter the major distinctions between federal and California anti-discrimination laws is discussed, including how the scope of potential liability in California is so much greater than at the federal level. We also examine how claims for harassment (discrimination's close companion) are weighed differently between federal and state courts, and how much higher the stakes are for individual managers in California, which allows for individual liability in certain circumstances. Finally, we will take a look at the state and federal administrative agencies responsible for enforcing the anti-discrimination laws and the damages available to employees who successfully bring suit.

California Anti-Discrimination Laws Surpass Federal Protections

Similar to federal anti-discrimination statutes, California's anti-discrimination legislation prohibits discrimination against individuals who belong to certain protected classes, including age (40 years and older), race, color, religion, sex, national origin, genetic information, veteran and military status, and disability. California's main anti-discrimination statute, the FEHA, goes well beyond the federal protected classes, however, and prohibits discrimination in employment because of an individual's sexual orientation, gender, gender identity and gender expression, marital status, and denial of medical, family, or pregnancy care leave. It also prohibits retaliation for protesting illegal discrimination related to one or more of these categories. Both state and federal anti-discrimination statutes not only protect those individuals who themselves belong to these protected classes, but also individuals who are perceived to be members of one or more of these classes or who have an association with a person who has, or is perceived to have, one or more of these characteristics. Therefore, to do business in California, employers must remember to amend or support their policies and practices to recognize the greater scope of potential protected classes.

Here are some key differences between California and federal law.

More Employers Are Covered under California Law than Federal Law

California's laws reach more employers than their federal counterparts. In particular, the FEHA applies to employers who employ five or more people, a significantly smaller number than federal anti-discrimination statutes, like Title VII and the ADA, which typically apply to employers who employ 15 or more people (20 or more people under the ADEA).

Sexual Orientation Discrimination Prohibited under California Law

There are no federal laws prohibiting discrimination on the basis of an individual's sexual orientation. California, however, protects employees within the state from discrimination based on their actual or perceived sexual orientation. "Sexual orientation" is defined by the FEHA as "heterosexuality, homosexuality, and bisexuality." Religious nonprofit organizations (for example, churches, synagogues, mosques) and those employers with four or fewer employees are exempt from the state's sexual orientation anti-discrimination statutes.

The FEHA Prohibits Discrimination Based on Gender, Gender Identity, and Gender Expression

On January 1, 2012, the FEHA was amended to clarify that gender, gender identity, and gender expression are protected classes. The FEHA defines gender expression as a person's gender-related appearance and behavior, whether or not said appearance or behavior is stereotypically associated with the person's sex at birth. California law protects an employee's right to appear or dress consistently with his or her gender identity or gender expression; however, employers can still require that the employee adhere to reasonable workplace dress and grooming standards.

Federal law does not currently extend anti-discrimination protections based on a person's gender, gender identity, or gender expression, but the EEOC appears to be pushing Congress in that direction. In April 2012, the EEOC ruled in *Macy v. Holder* (an internal EEOC administrative decision) that intentional discrimination based on gender identity, change of sex, or transgender status is prohibited under Title VII, even though these categories are not contained in the text of Title VII. In its decision, the EEOC asserted that Title VII's prohibition against sex discrimination is not limited to biological sex:

> When an employer discriminates against someone because the person is transgender, the employer has engaged in disparate treatment "related to the sex of the victim." . . . This is true regardless of whether an employer discriminates against an employee because the individual has expressed his or her gender in a non-stereotypical fashion, because the employer is uncomfortable with the fact that the person has transitioned or is in the process of transitioning from one gender to another, or because the employer simply does not like that the person is identifying as a transgender person."

The *Macy v. Holden* decision will likely serve as a roadmap for future litigants, paving the way for federal courts to use Title VII to prohibit gender identity discrimination. So what does this mean for California employers, primarily that now they may face potential liability under both California and federal law for alleged gender, gender identity, or gender expression discrimination?

Marital Status Discrimination

California law prohibits discrimination on the basis of marital status, unless based on a bona fide occupational qualification or on applicable security regulations established by the United States or the state of California. (A "bona fide occupational qualification," sometimes referred to as a "BFOQ," is an inherent characteristic or trait required by a particular position.) Marital status is defined by the FEHA as an individual's state of marriage, non-marriage, divorce or dissolution, separation, widowhood, annulment, or other marital status. Often, marital status discrimination is implicated when an employer automatically applies anti-nepotism policies (for example, precluding a married couple from reporting to the same supervisor) without any consideration of the particular circumstances to determine if spouses can work in the same department without issue or otherwise be accommodated.

An employer must make a reasonable attempt to provide its California employees with opportunities equal to those available to other employees, regardless of their marital status.

Under California law, registered domestic partners in the state are provided with the same rights, benefits, and protections of married couples under California law. Therefore, by way of extension, the protections afforded by the FEHA's anti-discrimination provisions regarding an individual's marital status also apply to those individuals who participate in a domestic partnership.

In contrast, under federal law as of the date of this book, registered domestic partners do not enjoy the rights and benefits of married couples.

One more point regarding marriage rights bears mentioning: A California law (SB 757) that went into effect on January 1, 2013, requires health care service plans and insurance policies to provide coverage to domestic partners of employees equal to coverage provided to spouses of employees. An employer's health care services plan cannot discriminate in coverage based on whether the spouse or domestic partner is of a different sex or the same sex as the employee. Based on these additional protections afforded to registered domestic partners in the state, prudence dictates that California employers audit the health care and insurance plans available to their employees in the state to make sure they are in compliance with the new law and that employees who belong to domestic partnerships have the same access to benefits as married couples.

Sex Discrimination—California's Expanded Definition of "Sex"

Enacted in fall 2012, AB 2386 expands its already broad definition of sex under the FEHA. True to form, the FEHA's definition of sex was already far more expansive than its federal counterpart, including in its definition of gender, pregnancy, childbirth, and medical conditions related to pregnancy or childbirth. Now California law defines sex to include all of the above plus breast-feeding or medical conditions related to breast-feeding.

The whole basis of the 2012 amendment was to codify a 2009 decision issued by the California Fair Employment and Housing

Commission (FEHC) in *Department of Fair Employment and Housing v. Acosta Tacos*, FEHC Precedential Decision 09-03P, 2009. In that case, the company returned an employee to work after she gave birth. When the owner learned that the employee was breast-feeding during her break, he prohibited the employee from continuing the practice. He sent her home and told her that he would call her back to work after she stopped breast-feeding, but the employee complained that she could not afford to be off work until she stopped breast-feeding. Instead of trying to work with the employee, the company fired her. After the employee filed a complaint with the FEHC, the agency found in her favor and determined the company violated the law. In its finding, the FEHC ruled that "breastfeeding is an activity intrinsic to the female sex." It also found that "termination in violation of complainant's right to return to work from pregnancy disability leave because she was still breastfeeding was discrimination on the basis of sex, a violation of [the FEHA]."

The bottom line here is that breast-feeding employees are a protected class, and California employers cannot subject these employees to any adverse employment action because they are breast-feeding. This is in addition to the state's requirement that private employers of all sizes make reasonable efforts to provide employees with the use of a room or other location, other than a toilet stall, in close proximity to the employees' work area, for employees to express milk in private.

Age Discrimination—A Varied Burden of Proof

Though both federal and California law protect individuals age 40 and over from discrimination on the basis of age in the employment setting, the two differ in a couple of areas.

Federal and California law differ when it comes to what an employer may consider when making termination decisions. Under federal law, employment decisions based on factors that merely correlate with age, like salary or years of service, do not *per se* constitute treatment based on age. For example, in the case of *Hazen Paper Co. v. Biggins* (1993), the U.S. Supreme Court held that age and years of service are analytically distinct, so that an employer could take account of one while ignoring the other, and the decision based on years of service is thus not necessarily age-based. In other words, a company *may* under the ADEA reasonably consider terminating higher-paid employees as a way to save money, even though statistically the higher-paid employees are likely to be older.

In contrast, the California legislature passed a law (CA Gov. Code 12941.1, overturning a state appellate court decision) declaring that "the use of salary as the basis for differentiating between employees when terminating employment may be found to constitute age discrimination if that use of criterion adversely impacts older workers as a group." Therefore, companies must be very careful and do a full impact analysis before engaging in layoffs.

Mandatory retirement is also a hot button issue in both federal and state jurisdictions. Both the ADEA and the FEHA prohibit employers from instituting a mandatory retirement age, even if retirement is authorized by the terms of a seniority plan or an employee benefits plan. Whereas federal law contains multiple exceptions to this general rule, California effectively has only three:

- A professional medical corporation may require any physician who is at least 70 years of age employed by the corporation to retire, if the corporation's bylaws provide for compulsory retirement;
- An employer may require mandatory retirement of any employee who is at least age 65 and who, for the two years preceding retirement, held a bona fide executive or high policy-making position, if the employee is immediately entitled to a nonforfeitable annual retirement benefit of at least $27,000; and
- Colleges and universities may require mandatory retirement at age 70 for tenured faculty.

For the latter exception to apply, the FEHA also requires that the institution have a policy permitting reemployment of these individuals on a year-to-year basis.

Disability Discrimination—The State and Federal Divide

Both federal and California law prohibit discrimination based on disability, but California's definition of what constitutes a disability embodies the adage "less is more." An individual is considered disabled under the FEHA if he or she is "limited" in one or more major life

activities, including physical, mental, and social activities and working, rather than substantially limited in those activities as required
under the federal ADA. The FEHA also extends protections to a person who has a record of such an impairment; is regarded or treated
as having an impairment; is regarded or treated as having a condition
that is not presently disabling, but may become disabling; or has *any*
health impairment that requires special education or related services.
Furthermore, California law prohibits not only disability discrimination but also discrimination against employees based on a medical condition (defined as either a health impairment that is related to or associated with a diagnosis of cancer, a record or history of cancer, or an
individual's genetic characteristics).

The FEHA also requires California employers to provide reasonable
accommodation to an employee or job applicant with a disability, unless doing so would cause undue hardship to the business operations.
In the process of determining a reasonable accommodation, the FEHA
requires that the employer enter into a timely, good faith interactive
process to determine if there is a reasonable accommodation that would
allow the individual to obtain or maintain employment.

So far, all of this matches up with the employer's requirements
under the ADA. The difference is that if an employer in California fails
to engage in the interactive process or to offer a reasonable accommodation, the employer could get hit with separate causes of action
under the FEHA for failure to engage in the interactive process and/
or failure to reasonably accommodate, apart from a claim of FEHA disability discrimination. Therefore, even if a company can show that an
employee's disability prevents that employee from doing his or her job,
and that no reasonable accommodation exists, the employer can still
be sued, and *lose*, if it failed to engage in the interactive process. No
such independent cause of action exists under federal law.

Although the FEHA does not provide detail regarding all that is
required to engage in a good faith interactive process, at the very least
California employers must meet with the employee to discuss what
reasonable accommodations can be made, if any, as soon as the employer is put on notice of a possible disability. An employer's obligation
under the FEHA to engage in an interactive process is triggered when
the employee gives the employer notice of the disability and a desire
for a reasonable accommodation. One case (*Reese v. Barton Healthcare*

Systems, 2010) illustrates this principle well. In the *Reese* case, the employer waited to engage in the first interactive process concerning the plaintiff's disability until the day the employee was suspended for performance problems. Unfortunately, this was several months after the employee had first requested an accommodation. Given the lack of discussions with the employee for over seven months and the timing of scheduling an interactive process meeting immediately after a potentially pretextual suspension, the court held that the plaintiff presented sufficient evidence for a reasonable juror to conclude that the company did not timely engage in the interactive process in good faith.

Considering the stringent standards and more expansive liability for failing to timely meet with employees to discuss possible reasonable accommodation for a wider array of disabilities and medical conditions, best practices dictate that California employers establish clear protocols to begin the interactive process as soon as they are put on notice of a possible disability of an employee and that employers contemporaneously document these discussions to demonstrate their efforts should the employee later file a lawsuit.

California's Expanded Accommodation of Religion

Both California and federal anti-discrimination laws prohibit discrimination based on religion. However, the FEHA's protections for accommodation of an individual's religious affiliation were expanded with the passage of AB 1964—a California law that went into effect January 1, 2013. The law clarified that a religious grooming practice and wearing religious clothing are protected under the FEHA. The new statute also defines religious creed as all aspects of religious belief, observance, and practice, including religious dress and grooming practices. The term religious dress practice is defined under the statute as the wearing or carrying of religious clothing, head or face covering, jewelry, artifacts, and any other item that is part of the observance by an individual of his or her religious creed. Religious grooming practice includes all forms of head, facial, and body hair that are part of the observance by an individual of his or her religious creed.

CalGINA—Broader Take on Genetic Anti-Discrimination Legislation

The California Genetic Information Nondiscrimination Act (CalGINA), which took effect on January 1, 2012, provides broader protections from genetic discrimination than does the federal GINA of 2008, which is limited to employment and health insurance coverage. Moreover, whereas GINA applies only to employers with 15 or more employees, CalGINA expands the pool of California employers required to comply with its provisions to include those persons and entities employing at least five employees.

CalGINA effectively amended the FEHA to include "genetic information" on the list of protected categories contained in the latter statute. Based on this inclusion, an employer cannot refuse to hire or employ a person, exclude a person from a training program, harass or discharge a person from employment, or otherwise discriminate against a person in compensation or in terms, conditions, or privileges of employment based on an individual's genetic tests, the genetic tests of family members of the individual, or the manifestation of a disease or disorder in family members of the individual.

Obesity—A New Protected Class on the Horizon

Although an individual's weight is not currently a protected class under either federal or California anti-discrimination laws, this might change in the near future. Since 2008, the EEOC has filed multiple civil actions against employers arguing that their alleged discrimination against morbidly obese employees violated the ADA. Whether obesity is eventually recognized as a disability under federal law, or becomes a protected category in its own right, California is already well ahead in offering overweight employees the same measure of job protection.

Traditionally, California courts held that although weight may qualify as a protected disability within the meaning of the FEHA, medical evidence must first show that the excessive weight was the result of a physiological condition affecting one or more basic bodily symptoms and limiting a major life activity. This standard was set by the California Supreme Court when it relied on the more stringent language in the ADA to interpret the FEHA and the EEOC's then-apparent position that obesity did not constitute a qualifying disability absent proof of an underlying physiological condition under federal law. The Supreme Court later backed away from its earlier position regarding the scope of the FEHA, holding that the FEHA requires a limitation on a major life activity, but does not require, as does the ADA, a "substantial limitation."

Given broader interpretation of the FEHA, coupled with the EEOC's recent position interpreting the provisions of the ADA to include "severe obesity" as a disability under the ADA without any proof of a physiological basis for it (as discussed above), it is reasonable to conclude that California courts will begin holding or finding that morbid obesity is a disability, even absent an underlying physiological condition.

Employers must also be aware that local ordinances in some California cities already expressly prohibit employment discrimination based on weight. For example, as discussed below in the section, "Local Anti-Discrimination Ordinances," the San Francisco Police Code makes it unlawful for an employer with more than five employees to fail or refuse to hire, discharge, or otherwise discriminate against individuals because of an employee's, independent contractor's, or applicant's actual or perceived weight.

Scope of Liability—The Stakes Are Raised in California

Most federal courts have interpreted federal anti-discrimination statutes, such as Title VII and the ADA, to preclude personal liability for individual supervisors. The California Supreme Court and appellate courts have followed the federal courts' lead for the most part, holding that supervisors cannot be personally liable for discrimination under the ADA in personnel decisions, nor can they be sued for wrongful termination in violation of public policy if the underlying public policy is the anti-discrimination provisions of the FEHA. Similarly, California Supreme Court precedent holds that individual supervisors may not be held personally liable for retaliation under the FEHA.

When it comes to harassment claims, however, all bets are off. By statute, Section 12940 of the FEHA specifically provides for personal liability in harassment claims for employers *and* "any person acting as an agent of an employer, directly or indirectly." California courts interpret this to mean that an individual supervisor *can* be held personally liable for harassment under the FEHA. By way of contrast, mere inaction by a non-harassing supervisor does not constitute separate harassment. Under the law, a supervisor who simply fails to take action to prevent the sexual harassment of another employee cannot be found personally liable as an aider and abettor of the harasser or the employer, or as an agent of the employer.

The California Supreme Court examined the scope of an individual supervisor's personal liability for FEHA harassment in the case of *Roby v. McKesson* (2009). In the case, a long-time employee sued her former employer for disability discrimination and her individual supervisor for disability-based harassment after her former supervisor disciplined and discharged her for excessive absenteeism. The employee claimed that her supervisor's behavior included making negative comments about the employee's body odor in front of other workers, calling her "disgusting" because of sores on her arms and her excessive sweating, openly snubbing the employee by refusing to respond to her greetings, ignoring her at staff meetings, requiring the employee to answer phones during a company holiday party, and reprimanding the employee in front of others.

The Supreme Court ultimately sided with the employee, expanding the scope of evidence that can be considered by the court and the jury in determining whether an individual supervisor may be found personally liable for harassment. All of a supervisor's conduct, even conduct that would otherwise be considered official "managerial activities" made on behalf of the company, can also be considered "hostile social interactions in the workplace" (for example, shunning an employee at staff meetings, reprimanding the employee in front of others), and hence will be considered when evaluating a supervisor's potential individual liability for harassment.

Agencies Responsible for Addressing Illegal Discrimination

The vast majority of the anti-discrimination laws in California are enforced by two agencies—the federal EEOC and the California DFEH. Employees may use the administrative functions of either the DFEH or the EEOC, or both, for resolution of their complaint.

When a complaint is filed, information is requested from the company, and an investigation is started. This process, often involving the employer's writing a statement of its position and providing any additional information requested by the agency, can take many months. Disgruntled current or former employees who don't have the patience to wait, however, can immediately request a right-to-sue notice from the DFEH and file a civil lawsuit. Though the EEOC does not typically provide a right-to-sue letter on request, it will dismiss a charge (allowing suit) if the DFEH does so first.

The FEHA, which is enforced by the DFEH, requires an aggrieved applicant or employee to file a complaint with the DFEH within one year of the alleged violation. Under federal law, a complainant must file a charge with the EEOC within 180 calendar days of the alleged violation. The 180-calendar-day filing deadline is extended to 300 calendar days if a state or local agency enforces a law that prohibits employment discrimination on the same basis.

Under California law, a complainant has one year from the date the right-to-sue letter is issued to file a civil lawsuit. In contrast, an individual has only 90 days from receipt of a right-to-sue letter from the EEOC to file a civil lawsuit for claims under Title VII, the ADA, the ADEA, or the GINA. Failure to file a charge or request a right-to-sue letter within the statutory period is typically a bar to the employee's claim, except in the case of a claim under the ADEA, which prohibits age discrimination. The ADEA only requires that an employee wait 60 days after filing a charge with the EEOC before filing a civil lawsuit; a determination or right-to-sue letter is not necessary.

Damages for Violation of Anti-Discrimination Laws May Vary

Under federal anti-discrimination laws, damages are either capped or limited to double the actual damages, depending on the nature of the claim and the number of employees working for the employer at the time. Damages under the federal GINA are the same as those previously stated and are also limited to reinstatement, hiring, promotion, back pay, injunctive relief, and pecuniary and nonpecuniary damages (including compensatory and punitive damages, together capped at between $50,000 and $300,000, depending on the size of the employer). In contrast, California law allows plaintiffs who have filed suit under the FEHA, including CalGINA, to recover unlimited monetary damages, such as back pay, future lost earnings, emotional distress damages, punitive damages, and attorney fees and costs, including expert witness fees.

Local Anti-Discrimination Ordinances

Any commentary on California anti-discrimination legislation would not be complete without mention of the numerous California counties and cities that have also jumped on the bandwagon of banning certain conduct in the employment setting. In addition to ensuring compliance with state and federal anti-discrimination laws, California employers with operations or employees working in certain cities in the Golden State must review local ordinances to ensure compliance with the local anti-discrimination legislation. See the textbox for a few local ordinances to keep on your radar.

San Francisco Police Code

Section 3303 of the San Francisco Police Code makes it unlawful for an employer with more than five employees to fail or refuse to hire, discharge, or otherwise discriminate against individuals because of an employee's, independent contractor's, or applicant's actual or perceived weight. The crux of it is that if you have employees working in the city of San Francisco, you may be on the receiving end of a lawsuit if an employee claims weight discrimination, regardless of the existence of any underlying physiological condition.

Santa Cruz Municipal Code

In similar vein to San Francisco's ban on weight discrimination, Santa Cruz has also codified its anti-discrimination stance, including adding height, weight, and physical characteristics to the list of protected categories under the Santa Cruz Municipal Code prohibiting discrimination (Section 9.83.010). The ordinance applies to employers that regularly employ five or more individuals, not including the employer's parents, spouse, or children.

San Diego Human Dignity Ordinance

In an effort to provide greater protections for the civil rights of individuals in the transgender community, the San Diego City Council amended the city's Human Dignity Ordinance in 2003 to include protections for transgender individuals in employment, housing, public accommodations, and education. The ordinance applies to private employers with five or more persons, excluding religious organizations and their schools.

California's Many Leave Laws:

Does Anyone Even Have to Work Anymore?

So, we've now discussed how to employ people in California. Now let's turn our attention to the numerous ways the law allows those very same employees to *avoid* working. That's right—we're talking protected leave of absence laws.

At the federal level, leave of absence laws are fairly limited in number (there are effectively two primary laws) and apply only to larger companies (those with 50 or more employees) or to companies that employ a specific type of employee (those who are in the military). Though the federal leave laws are often difficult to administer, the underlying purpose of the laws was to allow employees, in certain limited circumstances, the right to take time off from work without fear of losing their jobs.

California, however, was simply not satisfied with the rights given by the federal government. Therefore, as with both its complex wage and hour laws and its expansive anti-discrimination statutes, California decided to create a smorgasbord of different employee leave rights that cover a variety of circumstances far outside anything considered by the federal government. Further, not only are there significantly more state and local laws in play, but the burdens imposed by those laws must be coordinated with the rights granted by the federal laws. This all amounts to an administrative nightmare for most companies that, ultimately, are just hoping that enough workers show up every day to get the job done.

Because of the inherent complexity of the numerous different leave rights imposed by California, a look at how the various laws compare (and sometime contrast) with the federal rights given to employees is warranted. This is followed by a discussion on how companies can try to get a handle on administering the laws, including taking suggestions from two experienced HR professionals on what worked for them.

The Feds Set the Floor—FMLA and USERRA

There are probably few employers—or even workers—who are un-aware of the Family and Medical Leave Act (FMLA). Enacted in 1993, the FMLA protects employees who are sick, have to care for a loved one who is sick, or need to take time off for the birth of or bonding with a new child. The law guaranteed that employees could take up to 12 weeks of leave for these purposes, and set up a regulatory process for employers and workers to follow. The law applies to employers with 50 or more employees within 75 miles of an employer worksite. Employees are eligible to take FMLA leave only if they have worked at least 1,250 hours in the 12 months prior to taking a leave of absence. Of note, the 12-month period need not be consecutive as employees are entitled to have intermittent periods of work aggregated to qualify for FMLA leave. A serious health condition that entitles an employee to leave under the FMLA is one that requires in-patient care or con-tinuing treatment by a health care provider.

In 2008, the FMLA was amended to take into account the needs of employees whose family members serve in the armed forces and Reserves. The "military leave" amendments now also permit 12 weeks of leave for short-notice deployment, military events, counseling, and making legal and financial arrangements due to service member's ab-sence, as well as up to 26 weeks to care for ill or injured returning service members or veterans of the armed services.

Approximately one year after the FMLA was passed, Congress en-acted the Uniformed Services Employment and Reemployment Rights

Act (USERRA). A response to the needs of reservists during the first Gulf War, USERRA aims to protect the jobs of employees who volunteer to serve in the armed forces. USERRA applies to all employers and employees regardless of length of employment and provides for up to five years of leave for employees who are on deployment. With certain specific exceptions accounting for reductions in force, USERRA generally guarantees eligible employees with reemployment and also entitles those individuals to the position that they would have attained but for the fulfillment of their military obligations.

The FMLA and USERRA (along with a dash of influence from the Americans with Disabilities Act), make up the only major federal leave laws that apply to employees across the country. These federal laws, of course, represent the "floor" of protection—meaning companies must adhere to these laws regardless of whether the states in which they are operating have enacted additional legislation governing leaves of absence. Unlike many states that found the federal floor sufficient to protect their citizens, California chose instead to use the FMLA and USERRA as simply a starting point, enacting numerous additional leave laws that provide employee protections in a variety of different situations.

California's Numerous Leave Laws

Understanding and abiding by federal leave laws is only the beginning of your compliance obligations if your organization maintains operations in California. In addition to the federal laws at issue, California employers must be aware of the state-specific leave obligations that are dispersed across California's Government Code, Labor Code, Unemployment Insurance Code, and Elections Code. A key to tackling these laws is recognition that *all* the laws apply *in addition* to the federal laws.

California Family Rights Act: California's Counterpart to the FMLA

The FMLA and the California Family Rights Act (CFRA) are largely similar in scope and implementation. In fact, an unwary employer moving into California for the first time might be fooled into thinking that they are identical. For example, like the FMLA, the CFRA applies to employers with 50 or more employees within 75 miles of an employer worksite, and the employee must also have worked at least 1,250 hours during the 12-month period preceding the leave of absence. What is considered a "serious health condition" under the CFRA is also similar to the requirements of the FMLA but with several key distinctions. Like the FMLA, where the serious health condition is one involving continuing treatment, the employee must also show that he or she experienced a period of incapacity of more than three consecutive days along with subsequent treatment by a health care provider.

Unfortunately, as with most California laws, the devil is in the details of how the two laws differ. Some of the most significant differences are in the notice and certifications requirements of the FMLA and the CFRA, which could lead a company, without any ill-motive whatsoever, to engage in illegal activity and subject itself to significant liability.

First, pursuant to the FMLA, an employer may request a diagnosis identifying the employee's serious health condition at issue. That type of request is prohibited under the CFRA, in which it is up to the employee's discretion to provide the diagnosis requiring the leave. This is a significant departure from the type of certification information employers may demand under the FMLA. In California, it is *illegal* to demand a diagnosis or description of the course of treatment from an employee. Therefore, under the CFRA, an employer receiving a certification from an employee is only entitled to know (a) when the serious health condition began if the date is known, (b) the likely length of the leave, and (c) a statement from a health care provider that the employee is unable to work due to his or her serious health condition. An employee may disclose the condition voluntarily, but the company has no right to ask or expect to learn about it.

The second major difference between the FMLA and the CFRA is that the distinctions in the certification process extend to the recertification of leaves of absence. Under the FMLA, an employer may require an employee to obtain recertification if the employee wishes to extend the leave beyond the period originally designated by the employee's health care provider. Employers have the same right to recertification under the CFRA if the employee seeks to extend the leave of absence. However, the employer is entitled to no additional information about the serious health condition than what was provided at the initial certification.

Third, the CFRA, like the FMLA, permits employers that doubt the validity of the employee's medical certification to require a second or third opinion by a physician designated and paid for by the employer. The third opinion may be ordered only when the first and second opinions conflict, in which case the third opinion is final and binding. Unlike the FMLA, however, the CFRA contains no corresponding regulation allowing for second and third opinions when it comes to certifications about family members—meaning employers must accept the medical certification of a family member even when the employer questions the validity or accuracy of the certification.

Fourth, the CFRA, unlike the FMLA, permits leave for an employee to care for a registered domestic partner who is suffering from a serious health condition. To qualify as registered domestic partners, both individuals must file a declaration of partnership with the California Secretary of State attesting that they meet the requirements spelled out in California Family Code Section 297(b). Of note, because a right to leave to care for a domestic partner is not found in the FMLA, leaves of this nature under the CFRA do not run concurrently with the FMLA. This could lead to an individual in a domestic partnership getting double leave—12 weeks under the CFRA to care for a domestic partner and 12 weeks under the FMLA for himself or herself.

Finally, the CFRA does not cover pregnancy disability as a serious health condition, as California has a separate law for pregnancy-related disability leave (discussed in the next section). This diverges from the FMLA, which does contain pre- and postnatal incapacity within its definition of a serious health condition. The CFRA does, however, cover well-baby bonding time. Therefore, because of California's separate laws for well-baby bonding time and pregnancy-related disability, "maternity leave" has the potential to last up to seven months.

California Pregnancy Disability Leave Law

California's Pregnancy Disability Leave Law (PDLL) is a Fair Employment and Housing Act (FEHA) provision that makes it unlawful for an employer to refuse to allow female employees who are disabled by pregnancy, childbirth, or a related medical condition to take a leave for a reasonable period of time not to exceed four months. Unlike the FMLA and the CFRA, the PDLL applies from day one of employment and applies to all employees, regardless of tenure or status. Of note, leave taken under the PDLL does *not* run concurrently with leave taken under the CFRA (although the FMLA can be run concurrently).

Employees eligible for PDLL may elect to use paid time off that is offered by the employer such as vacation time, paid sick days, or paid personal days. Employers should also be aware that, unlike the CFRA and the FMLA, the PDLL requires that an employee be returned to the *same* position held by the employee prior to the leave. Returning an employee to a *similar* position to the one held prior to taking the leave (allowed by the CFRA and the FMLA) is *not* sufficient to comply with the statute.

Keeping track of an employee's rights under the various statutes can be complicated. Table 4.1 lays out the differences and interplay between the FMLA, the CFRA, and the California PDLL.

By combining leaves under the FMLA, the CFRA, and the PDLL, employees in California may take more pregnancy-related leave—up to seven months—than what is permitted under each of the statutes. For example, an employee who is entitled to only the FMLA may be put on bed rest one month before her due date. As a result, the employee would only have two months of protected leave after the birth for recovery or well-baby bonding time. An employee in California, however, could use

Table 4.1. Comparing FMLA with CFRA and PDLL

FMLA	CFRA and PDLL
Pregnancy is covered as a serious health condition. The law permits up to 12 weeks of disability or bonding time leave for eligible employees.	Under the CFRA, pregnancy is *not* covered as a serious health condition, but the CFRA permits up to 12 weeks of bonding time leave for eligible employees.
	The PDLL entitles every employee to up to four months of pregnancy-related disability leave regardless of length of employment. The four-month leave period is equivalent to the number of hours an employee would regularly work in 17⅓ weeks. For instance, a full-time employee who works 40 hours per week is entitled to 693 hours of leave. Employees who work more or less than that are entitled to a *pro rata* or proportional amount of leave.
FMLA leave for a pregnancy-related disability runs concurrently with the PDLL but not with the CFRA.	Bonding time leave under the CFRA does not run concurrently with disability leave under the PDLL.

the PDLL for the month of leave prior to her due date and still have a full 12 weeks of well-baby bonding time remaining under the CFRA.

Further, under a 2013 ruling by the California Court of Appeals in *Sanchez v. Swissport, Inc.*, even after an employee exhausts all her leave under the PDLL and the CFRA/FMLA, she may be entitled to even *more* leave if the need for leave is based on a pregnancy-related disability. This is due to the 2012 amendments to the FEHA's disability standards, which were expanded to explicitly include pregnancy-related disabilities as conditions for which a reasonable accommodation (including additional leave) may be required. In other words, under California law, seven months of leave may just be the beginning, instead of signaling the end, of state-mandated maternity leave.

California Paid Family Leave

California's Paid Family Leave (PFL) law was designed to be a temporary family disability insurance program within the existing state disability insurance program. The program provides up to six weeks of wage replacement to eligible employees who take a leave to care for a seriously ill child, spouse, parent, or domestic partner, or to bond with a minor child who is within one year of birth. In the case of foster care or adoption, the time off to bond must be within one year of the placement of the child. Effective July 1, 2014, benefits are expanded to include time off to care for a seriously ill grandparent, grandchild, sibling, or parent-in-law. Payments to eligible employees are made through California's State Disability Fund, and eligibility is determined by the Employment Development Department. The PFL does not provide for protected leave in that it does not entitle employees to job protection or reinstatement rights. Moreover, the PFL leave runs concurrently with both FMLA and CFRA.

Of interest, though the PFL is not a leave law in itself, it is being touted by some in Congress as a model to bring a paid leave component to the FMLA.

Kin Care Leave

California's kin care leave law permits employees to use a designated amount of "accrued and available" sick leave to care for a sick child, spouse, parent, or domestic partner. The statute only applies to employers that provide a designated amount of paid sick leave to their employees. Therefore, employers that provide an unlimited, or uncapped, number of paid sick leave days are not subject to the statute. The employer may designate the number of kin care days that employees may take, but the designated amount may not be less than the number of paid sick leave days that an employee would accrue during a six-month period. For example, if an employee accrues two sick days per month, then the employer's kin care leave policy may set a cap of no less than 12 days.

Domestic Violence and Sexual Assault Victims Leave

California's Domestic Violence and Sexual Assault Victims Leave law applies to employers with 25 or more employees and prohibits the termination of, or discrimination against, an employee who is a victim of domestic violence or of sexual assault. Eligible employees are entitled to take an unpaid leave of absence to obtain relief to ensure the health, safety, or welfare of the employee or his or her family and to attend judicial proceedings related to the crime. Employees may take this leave for the following reasons:

- To seek medical attention for injuries caused by domestic violence or sexual assault.
- To obtain services from a domestic violence shelter, program, or rape crisis center as a result of domestic violence or sexual assault.
- To obtain psychological counseling related to an experience of domestic violence or sexual assault.
- To participate in safety planning and take other actions to increase safety from future domestic violence or sexual assault, including temporary or permanent relocation.

Crime Victims Leave

California's Crime Victims Leave law is intended to permit employees to attend judicial proceedings related to a crime committed against the employee or a member of the employee's immediate family. An employee is eligible for this leave if he or she was the victim of a crime or if a crime was committed against the employee's spouse, child, sibling or step-sibling, parent or step-parent, registered domestic partner, or the child of a registered domestic partner. An employee taking this leave must provide the employer with documentation evidencing the judicial proceedings that the employee wishes to attend.

Emergency Duties Leave Laws

California law prohibits employers from discharging or discriminating against employees who take time off to perform emergency duties as volunteer firefighters, reserve peace officers, or emergency rescue personnel. Moreover, employers with 50 or more employees must permit individuals who are also volunteer firefighters to take temporary leaves of absence for the purpose of engaging in fire or law enforcement training of up to a maximum of 14 calendar days per year.

Family-School Partnership Act

California's Family-School Partnership Act prohibits termination or discrimination against employees who take time off to participate in activities at their child's school or day care facility. The law applies to employers with 25 or more employees working at the same location. Eligible employees include any parent, guardian, or grandparent having custody of a child in kindergarten or grades 1 through 12 or attending a licensed day care facility. Employees may take up to 40 hours of leave per year but not exceeding eight hours in any calendar month. The employee must give the employer reasonable notice and must use existing vacation, personal, or compensatory time, if any, for purposes of the planned time off. If paid time off (PTO)/vacation or personal time is not available to the employee, or if the employer does not offer such time to the employee, the employer must allow the employee to take the time off without pay.

California's "Time Off to Vote" Law

Employees who do not have sufficient time outside of their working hours to vote in a statewide election are entitled to leave that is sufficient for them to participate in the election. Employees are entitled to up to two hours of paid leave, although there is no limit on the amount of unpaid time an employee may take off to cast a ballot. The employee must provide at least two working days' notice that time off for voting is desired.

California Civil Air Patrol Employment Protection Act

The Civil Air Patrol (CAP) is a federally supported organization of civilian pilots that conducts disaster relief operations throughout the United States. California's CAP leave law prohibits employers from discriminating against or discharging from employment a member of the CAP because of the employee's membership in the CAP. The law also prohibits employers from hindering or preventing a member of the CAP from serving with the CAP during an emergency operations mission and requires employers to provide up to 10 days of unpaid leave to any eligible employee taking part in an emergency mission. Employers may not require that employees exhaust accrued paid time off to take CAP leave.

Organ and Bone Marrow Donor Leave Law

California's organ and bone marrow leave law, formally known as the Michelle Maykin Memorial Donation Protection Act, requires employers with 15 or more employees to grant leave of up to 30 business days per year to employees who are organ donors or leave of up to five business days per year to bone marrow donors. Employees must have worked for a period of at least 90 days prior to the leave to be eligible. The law also requires that leaves for organ or bone marrow donation not run concurrently with the FMLA or the CFRA. This means that leaves of absence under this law are in addition to the leaves an employee would be entitled to under the FMLA and the CFRA.

Federal and State Disability Laws—ADA, ADAAA, and FEHA

The Stated Goals of Disability Laws

The Americans with Disabilities Act (ADA), the ADA Amendments Act of 2008 (ADAAA), and the disability provisions of the FEHA are all focused on prohibiting discrimination against qualified individuals because of a disability. Unlike the leave laws, which entitle individuals to time off from work for various reasons, the disability laws are designed to encourage the employment and continued employment of individuals in need of an accommodation because of a qualifying disability. The type of injury or condition at issue, and how the injury or condition came about, is not the central focus of these laws. Regardless of how and where an injury or condition occurs, if it is or develops into a covered disability as defined by federal or state law, an employer's obligations kick in, and the analysis begins.

Coverage under the ADA and FEHA

The ADA applies only to employers with at least 15 employees, whereas the FEHA applies to all private employers with five or more employees. The ADA prohibits discrimination against applicants and employees who are "qualified individuals with a disability," and requires reasonable accommodations as long as the accommodations do not create an undue burden on the employer and the employee can perform his or her essential job functions with or without a reasonable accommodation. Similarly, the FEHA requires a reasonable accommodation as long as no hardship is created and the employee's essential job functions can be performed.

The ADA applies to employees if the disability at issue "substantially limits" a major life activity. The FEHA's definition of disability is broader in that it applies to any employee who has a physical or mental disability that limits a major life activity. The ADA and the FEHA became more compatible in 2008 with the passage of the ADAAA, which broadened the ADA's scope of coverage for employees with disabilities and moved closer to the protections afforded under the FEHA. The ADAAA reaffirmed the congressional intent for the definition of "disability" to be construed in favor of broad coverage of individuals and specifically overruled several Supreme Court decisions that had narrowed coverage under the ADA. In recent years, a large push was made by the U.S. Equal Employment Opportunity Commission and courts in many parts of the country to find that a period of extended leave could, in some circumstances, be deemed a reasonable accommodation under the ADA. Moreover, the FEHA specifically incorporates, adopts, and requires employers to comply with any protection afforded to the ADA that is broader than the protections contained in the FEHA.

Best Practices and Tips for Survival

Although knowing the myriad California leave laws is crucial, having a system in place to administer those laws is every bit as essential for a company doing business within the state. Most leave laws are "strict liability" laws, meaning that it makes no difference whether a company *intended* to deprive an employee of his or her rights; if leave was available, and the company interfered with an employee's right to take that leave, the company broke the law and is liable for damages. Because the most innocent of clerical mistakes carries the same penalty as the most craven of discriminatory motives, employers should take whatever steps are necessary to ensure full compliance.

One Size Does *Not* Fit All

Identifying best practices and implementing them will necessarily entail some level of customization for every organization. For example, John McQuade, an HR manager for the Dannon Company in the greater Salt Lake City area, approaches the creation and implementation of a core system to deal with leave issues as a company-wide process. "The creation of any company policy has to be a collaborative effort between human resources, company counsel, front line managers and any other departments or employees that are involved in a responding to a request for leave," he says.

McQuade also discourages reliance on any kind of one-size-fits-all approach to leave issues. Instead, McQuade encourages reviewing leave requests—whatever the reason may be—as a unique event. "Stepping away from a formulaic approach frees the company to engage in a more useful cost-benefit analysis of the immediate impact on business operations versus the long-term implications of granting or denying specific leave requests," he says. It may be more time consuming to approach administration of leave requests on an individualized basis, but considering the high risks involved, it is usually time well spent.

Follow a Three-Step Process

Pauline Gets, an HR professional in the San Francisco Bay area, takes a systematic three-step approach to organizing her company's leave program:

Step1. Assess the Requirements for Your Organization

"An organization must recognize that challenges for a human resource professional will vary based upon the type of organization they support," Gets says, whether it be national corporation versus single state, or a large organization versus a small, mom-and-pop type shop. For this reason, the HR department must make regular assessments as to which federal and state leave laws apply to the organization and which do not. Keep in mind that the organizational assessment is not a one-time project—companies change, and so do the state and federal laws that apply to them. An annual review of applicable laws and how the company administers them is an effective way to minimize risk.

Step 2. Conduct Basic Training

HR should coordinate the effort firm-wide to determine who needs to be trained . . . and then actually provide training. "This is different from posting notices on a bulletin board," Gets says. Instead, the process involves partnering with members of operations management and getting them to buy into what may otherwise be seen as a needless exercise that takes away from the actual business of the company. An effective one-two punch to gain the needed cooperation is (a) keeping the training basic and (b) reminding managers that under most leave laws, individual liability exists.

Keeping training simple is crucial. After all, Gets points out, it is your HR department that will manage the leave of absence, not your front-line supervisor. Front-line supervisors need to receive just enough information to know *when* to pass the issue along to human resources. To the extent possible, any leave requests—for whatever reason—should be managed by human resources. Obviously this may not work in every instance, but the more information on employee leave needs is centralized, the less chance there is for mistakes to be made.

Of course, training the HR staff to handle the centralized information is also important. Once human resources is made aware of a leave request, it must take control of the process. According to Gets, human resources should "capture the facts surrounding the absence, provide notice of leave provisions that are available to the employee and clearly outline for the employee how the leave process works." Then, once the leave starts, it is vital for human resources to maintain constant communication with supervisors who have employees out on leave.

Step 3. Maintain Strategic Coordination between Departments

Finally, though information regarding employees' need for leave should be funneled to human resources, overall implementation of the policies is a company-wide concern. Companies should think strategically about which departments other than human resources should be involved in coordinating an organizational response to a leave request. Gets notes, "Communication is critical not only between the human resource department and the field managers but also with the other departments within the organization such as payroll and safety." Prepare other departments for the unique challenges raised by a leave of absence such as:

- How is the employee on leave going to be paid?
- What insurance premiums need to be paid?
- Does the organization provide short- or long-term disability programs?
- Is there a state disability program available to the employee?

By involving departments such as payroll, benefits, and risk management in the overall leave of absence process, you create a firm-wide system that will hopefully be compliant not just with leave laws but with all employment laws.

Even More California Employment Laws to Worry About:

Why California HR Professionals Deserve the Big Bucks

Well, this is it. We've covered wage and hour laws, discrimination laws, and leave of absence laws. The big three . . . statutory and regulatory requirements that dictate the bulk of operating a business in California. What could be left? What more could California possibly throw at a company operating in the Golden State?

Well, since you ask . . . .

To illustrate many of the remaining laws, I'm going to let you shadow someone through her day as an HR manager. By taking you through a day-in-the-life of an HR professional in the Golden State, I hope to show just how versatile, how nimble, and how patient one must be to manage people working in California.

Therefore, I'd like to introduce you to "Sheila." Sheila will be our guide through the treacherous waters of California's laws and regulations concerning pre-employment inquires and drug testing, access to personnel files, employee record-keeping, prohibition on noncompetition/ nonsolicitation agreements, an employer's use of social media, eavesdropping on employees and customers, requirements to accommodate breast-feeding mothers in the workplace, and job reference liability.

From the start of Sheila's day to its exhausted end, sit back, relax, and enjoy the ride.

7:00 a.m. California Union Picketing Rights

It's 7:00 a.m. on Tuesday morning, and Sheila is on her way to her office at Golden Bear Industries (GBI). During her drive, Sheila listens to a news report on the local public radio station about a recent California Supreme Court case, *Ralphs Grocery Company v. United Food and Commercial Workers Union, Local 8*, which reaffirmed that in California a union has the right to picket a store, even if the location is private property. The court found that, under the state's Moscone Act (Section 527.3 of the California Code of Civil Procedure), a peaceful demonstration by a union could not be stopped, even though any similar nonunion activity could be prevented by the store's management. One of the talking heads on the radio questions whether the California Supreme Court had finally gone too far and interfered with federally controlled union laws. If so, the commentator suggested, the U.S. Supreme Court could step in and find the Moscone Act unconstitutional, or at least pre-empted by federal law. Shaking her head, Sheila is just glad GBI is union free—she has enough headaches as it is.

7:30 a.m. Limits on Employer
Inquires about Arrests and Convictions

Sheila arrives at work at 7:30 a.m. Although GBI's office hours don't officially begin until 8:30 a.m., Sheila knows she'll need this extra hour if she has any hope of getting through the pile of papers on her desk. Plus, by leaving her house a little earlier and using the drive-through at her favorite overpriced coffee bar on the way in, Sheila can bypass at least some of the horrendous rush-hour traffic.

Nonfat sugar-free almond-milk-macchiato in hand, Sheila boots up her computer and opens her e-mail. She's pleased to see only a dozen new messages, a modest number compared to the usual. This might turn out to be a good day.

After deleting her junk e-mails, Sheila reads an e-mail from Joe Hodson, GBI's warehouse supervisor, sent at 5:30 a.m. Sheila has been helping Joe in his search for a new receiving clerk.

Hey Sheila,

You know that guy (Seth) we had in yesterday for the interview, the one that used to work for Beautiful Plastics? Well, I really liked him, and he told me he's available to start right away. I was going to hire him on the spot. It's a good thing I didn't!

After the interview Jose came up to me and said he heard from his friend at Beautiful Plastics that Seth was charged with a DUI recently. I'm not sure if that's true, but if it is I got a real problem with that. Not that the receiving job requires driving or anything, but I just can't understand why anyone would put other people on the road in danger like that. It's wrong!

I want to give Seth a chance to explain himself, so I asked him to come in for a follow-up interview at 8:00 a.m. this morning. I figured I'd give you a heads up in case you want to sit in or something.

P.S. I haven't told Seth why I called him back in yet. I want to catch him off guard.

Joe

Sheila's heart races. "A chance to explain himself . . . 8:00 a.m." Joe's plan to grill Seth about his driving under the influence (DUI) arrest could present serious issues for GBI as a California employer. Sheila glances at the corner of her computer screen; it's 7:53 a.m. She grabs her hard hat and bolts toward the warehouse.

Most states don't prohibit employers from asking employees about prior arrests. The biggest limitation that most states place on arrest inquiries is allowing employees who have expunged or sealed records to refrain from acknowledging an arrest when asked by an employer. Likewise, no federal laws or regulations expressly forbid employers from inquiring about employee and applicant arrest records. The only federal guidance comes from the Equal Employment Opportunity Commission (EEOC), which warns that, under Title VII of the Civil Rights Act, employers *could* be liable for discrimination if they use arrest records in hiring or retention decisions and *if* using that information negatively effects applicants or employees based on a protected characteristic, such as sex or race. Thus, under federal law, questions about arrest records *could* be problematic, provided the inquiries cause harm based on a protected characteristic.

Although most states don't prohibit employers from asking questions about employees' arrest histories, California most certainly does. The California Labor Code (Sections 432.7 and 432.8) sets a bright line rule prohibiting employers from requiring an applicant to disclose information about any arrest or detention that didn't lead to a conviction, regardless of the alleged offense.

The Code also prohibits using an arrest or detention record (that did not result in a conviction) as a factor in making any employment decisions regarding current employees. California employers *can* ask an employee or applicant about an arrest for which the employee or applicant is on bail or for which he or she is awaiting trial—meaning that the issue hasn't been decided by the courts. In short, absent a conviction or a pending trial, California employers cannot promote, hire, or terminate employees or applicants for *any* arrest.

In addition to restrictions on questions about arrests, California employers cannot inquire about marijuana convictions that are more than two years old. California employers are also prohibited from inquiring about drug diversion programs.

Joe is obviously unaware of California's limitations on arrest inquires. And he definitely doesn't know that if he goes forward with his inquiry, Seth could sue GBI for damages, costs, and attorney fees under the Labor Code. The way Sheila sees it—and she'll definitely need to run this by her attorneys—Joe should not be asking Seth about this DUI. The only way Joe could get away with these questions is if Joe makes it clear that he is *not* asking Seth about (a) arrests that were prosecuted but did not result in convictions, or (b) marijuana convictions that are more than two years old.

Sheila arrives at the warehouse at 7:59 a.m., where she spots Joe shaking the hand of a man she doesn't recognize. It must be Seth. Sheila calmly strolls up just in the nick of time, trying not to breathe too hard, and asks to speak to Joe.

8:44 a.m. California Allows Drug Testing of Applicants and Employees under Certain Circumstances

It's 8:44 a.m. and the office is humming now. Sheila returns to her computer and finds another e-mail, this one from Sandy, the payroll manager.

> Sheila,
>
> Several of my employees came to me yesterday to complain that Jim Bradshaw, our new payroll clerk, came in yesterday stinking of marijuana.

I confronted Jim about this, and he said he has a medical marijuana prescription, so "there's nothing GBI can do to stop me."

Is that true???? Employees can't just come to work high, can they? I don't care what excuse he has!

Sandy

Sheila knows that, unlike most other states and the federal government, California's Medical Marijuana Program allows private citizens to possess and smoke medical marijuana for medicinal purposes.

Sheila also knows that California's Constitution provides a right to privacy for employees. Unlike the U.S. Constitution and the constitutions of many other states, California's constitutional right to privacy extends not only to government employees but to private employees as well.

Court decisions applying the California constitution have found that private employers can only perform drug testing on employees under certain circumstances. For example, the state allows pre-hire drug testing because employees have a reduced expectation of privacy before they begin a job with a new employer. Once an employee is hired, employers can test him or her if they have "reasonable suspicion" that the he or she is impaired. Finally, if an employee performs safety-sensitive work, his or her employer may perform random drug tests during his or her employment.

Sheila pauses to think about what this means for Jim and his medical marijuana card. Jim has already been hired, so he should have a higher expectation of privacy than an applicant to the company. Also, smoking medicinal pot is legal with a medical prescription. So couldn't Jim argue that he has a disability and that the Americans with Disabilities Act (or the California equivalent, the Fair Employment and Housing Act, or FEHA) requires GBI to let him smoke marijuana to accommodate his medical condition?

Sheila thumbs through an HR manual she has on her desk, thinking there has to be something about medical marijuana and drug testing. She finally finds what she's looking for under a discussion of Health and Safety Code Sections 11362.785, 72330.5, and 87013:

Although California has established a Medical Marijuana Program, employers have no obligation to accommodate medical marijuana use during the hours of employment.

Sandy will be pleased to know that Jim doesn't have the right to come to work stoned. Sheila e-mails Sandy to recommend that she carefully document her conversation with Jim and his admission that he smoked marijuana on the job. She then recommends that Sandy issue a "warning" indicating that Jim will be terminated if he continues his conduct. Although GBI could probably terminate Jim without issuing him a warning, Sheila's reluctant to make that recommendation given the sensitive issues at play.

Sheila looks at her watch; it's 9:45 a.m. She has just enough time to grab another cup of coffee before attending a webinar hosted by outside counsel.

10:00 a.m. California Allows Pre-Employment Background Checks and Fingerprints of Applicants for Employment in Sensitive Industries

Sheila logs in to the webinar at 10 a.m. just as GBI's outside employment counsel begins his presentation. The topic: pre-employment inquiries.

The attorney spends 45 minutes addressing drug testing, arrest inquires, and questions about marijuana convictions. Although Sheila wishes she'd had this training yesterday, in time for this morning's onslaught, she's pleased to learn that she came to the right decisions.

Then the attorney switches topics to medical and psychological examinations or inquiries of applicants. The attorney explains that, with limited exceptions for peace officers and other criminal justice employees, California generally prohibits employers from requiring employees and applicants to submit to medical or psychological examinations. The California FEHA also prevents employers from asking about mental or physical disabilities, medical conditions, or the nature or severity of various disabilities or medical conditions.

Despite these restrictions and the privacy interests of employees, employees in certain sensitive industries may be required to undergo background checks and to submit fingerprints. These employees include personnel at public and private schools, community college workers, health care professionals, child care providers, securities brokers, telephone workers, and employees of consumer reporting agencies.

11:30 a.m. Personnel and Payroll Files
Must Be Maintained for Three Years and
Made Available to Current and Former Employees

At 11:30 a.m. the mail is delivered. Sheila cringes at the sight of a letter from Malcott & Associates, LLC, a law firm that previously brought an employment lawsuit against GBI. "Please don't be a demand letter . . . please don't be a demand letter," Sheila mutters to herself as she takes a deep breath and tears open the letter—there's no point in delaying the inevitable.

Sheila's eyes dart back and forth down the page. She quickly realizes this isn't a demand letter but a request for personnel and payroll records. Sheila receives a few of these letters each year from various plaintiffs' attorneys on behalf of their clients. The letters spew boilerplate language from the California Labor Code about an employee's right to inspect his or her employment records, and demand that GBI turn over the records.

Though Sheila is relieved that this isn't a court summons or demand letter, her relief is tempered. She's seen enough of these personnel file requests to know they are often a precursor to litigation.

Although federal law requires employers to maintain personnel files, Sheila had never dealt with *requests* for personnel files until she moved to California. Sheila is aware of many other states that have personnel file retention and access requirements, but they all seem significantly less stringent than California. For example, some states, such as Georgia, have no laws on the books regarding access to personnel files. Other states, such as Florida, have no general laws regarding personnel files but do have requirements for limited industries. A third group, including Alabama, Arizona, Arkansas, and Colorado, requires only that *public* employers grant employees access to personnel files. Finally, a fourth group of states doesn't expressly allow access to files, but does provide that if an employee submits a written statement concerning a disagreement about information contained in his or her personnel file, that statement must accompany any transmittal or disclosure from the file or records made to a third party.

California's personnel file retention and production requirements are much more onerous. The files must be kept for a minimum of three years from the termination of employment and must be available for inspection by an employee or his or her agent within 30 days of a request. California Labor Code Section 1198.5 gives employers three options for making personnel files available to employees for inspection: (a) always keep a copy of the files at the employee's place of work; (b) make the records available at the work location within a reasonable time following an employee's request to inspect the records; or (c) store the personnel records offsite, but permit the employee to visit the offsite location to inspect them. Alternatively, an employer can simply make copies of the personnel records and transmit them to the employee following a request.

The following personnel records are not open to inspection: (a) investigations of a possible criminal offense; (b) reference letters; or (c) ratings, reports, or records that were obtained prior to the employee's employment, prepared by identifiable examination committee members, or obtained in connection with a promotional examination.

In addition to the requirements that employers maintain personnel files, California employers must also maintain payroll records for three years from the date of the last payroll entry. The Fair Labor Standards Act, which governs federal wage and hour law, also has a three-year requirement. In California, not only must payroll records be maintained, but California Labor Code Section 226(c) requires employers to allow inspection and/or copying of payroll records within 21 days of a request to view the files.

Failure to maintain and furnish personnel records as described above can lead to a penalty of $750, an action for injunctive relief to obtain compliance, and recovery of costs and reasonable attorney fees.

In addition to the requirements set forth above, Labor Code Sections 1174, 1197.5, and 1299 require employers to maintain (a) two years' worth of records of employee wages/rates, job classifications, and other employment terms; (b) certificates/permits on file for all minors working for the company; (c) a record of the names and addresses of all employees and the ages of all minors; and (d) payroll records showing the hours worked daily by and the wages paid to employees for at least three years. And Government Code 12946 requires employers to keep all job applications, personnel or employment referral records and files, applicant files, and terminated employee personnel files for at least two years.

As if the above requirements weren't complicated enough, California recently enacted Labor Code Section 2810.5 *requiring* employers to provide the following wage information to *all employees* at the time of hire: written notice of the rate or rates of pay and basis thereof, including overtime rates; any allowances claimed as part of the minimum wage; the name of the employer; and the employer's physical address. If any of the information in the notice changes during the employee's tenure with the company, employers must provide notice of that change, in writing, within seven days.

Sheila sends an e-mail to payroll requesting a copy of the former employee's payroll and personnel files. Once she receives the records, Sheila plans to forward them to her employment counsel for review to determine if GBI can withhold any of the documents and whether any of the documents might be of concern should litigation arise.

It's 12:38 p.m., and Sheila is starving. She has an interview with a prospective employee scheduled for 1 p.m. and needs to prepare for it. Sighing as she thinks of the succulent sandwiches served at a nearby deli, Sheila reaches into her desk for a power bar.

1:00 p.m. California Prohibits Noncompete and Nonsolicitation Agreements

Sheila is impressed by the job applicant, Frank Selma, during their 1 p.m. interview. Frank works for a Silicon Valley software company and would fit in perfectly as the director of GBI's IT department. There's only one problem: Frank signed an agreement not to compete with his employer for three years after he departs the company. He also agreed not to solicit his employer's other employees for three years. Frank is concerned that his employer will sue him if he leaves the company.

Having dealt with these noncompete agreements before, Sheila knows that Frank's agreement is unenforceable in California. Sheila sets out to put Frank's mind at ease.

Sheila explains to Frank that, unlike other states that often allow "reasonable" noncompete agreements, California has had a longstanding ban on these agreements, which is set forth in California Business and Profession Code Section 16600. The ban is rooted in the state's values of free competition, openness, and the concept that employees should not be restrained from engaging in a lawful profession, trade, or business of any kind.

The only narrow exceptions to the ban in California on nonsolicitation and noncompete agreements are for sales of the shares of a business or during the dissolution of a partnership. Neither of those exceptions applies in Frank's case. Therefore, if Frank's employer were to try to enforce a noncompete or nonsolicitation agreement against him, as a California employee, a court would have no choice but to invalidate the agreement. Or, if Frank wanted to go on the offensive, he could petition a court for a judgment declaring that the noncompete agreement is invalid and unenforceable.

Of course, California's prohibition against noncompete agreements would not extend to employees outside of California. But if an out-of-state employee were to sign a valid noncompete agreement in another state, and then move to California, a California court would probably find the agreement invalid. If the former employer insisted on enforcing the noncompete agreement, the employer could try to file an action to enforce the agreement in the state where the agreement was signed. But even if it was successful in its home state, there is no guarantee that the former employer would succeed in enforcing the order in a California court.

California's prohibition on noncompete and nonsolicitation agreements is precisely why GBI removed these agreements from its new-hire paperwork. Now GBI's agreements only provide limitations on the theft of clearly defined confidential, proprietary, and trade secret information—such clauses are allowed under California law.

Frank sounds persuaded, but since Sheila is not an attorney and, even if she was, does not want to be misunderstood as providing legal advice, she encourages him to consult with an attorney if he has any lingering doubts.

2:30 p.m. California Employers May Not Request the Social Media Passwords of Employees or Applicants

At 2:30 p.m. Sheila gathers managers from various departments in a conference room to discuss recent changes to the company's social media policy.

As Sheila explains to the managers, the company's practice of asking job applicants about their social media accounts during interviews must come to an end. Based on the personal privacy protections set forth in the state's constitution, the legislature recently enacted Labor Code Section 980, which prohibits employers and prospective employers from asking employees and applicants for their social media passwords. Companies are also prohibited from asking employees and applicants to access their social media in the presence of their employer, nor may companies ask them to "divulge" social media information. The company, Sheila explains, wants to make sure its interview questions cannot be construed as a violation of the statute.

Social media, as a potential HR tool, fascinates Sheila. From an HR perspective, the amount of information you can uncover on a site like Facebook—whether about applicants or current employees—is mind-blowingly powerful.

Sheila knows of several of GBI's competitors that, until recently, would request an applicant's Facebook password during the interview process and use it to log into the user's account. Sheila always felt uncomfortable with this practice and never did it herself. But as time went on, and as Sheila's competitors seemed to get a leg up by weeding out questionable applicants based on what they posted online, Sheila began to doubt her strategy. So Sheila began asking managers to integrate some simple questions about applicants' use of social media into the interview, such as which sites the applicant used and whether they kept their profiles "private."

Now that the legislature has put a ban on everything from requesting applicants' passwords to asking applicants to divulge information about their social media, it's going to put a chill on the questions Sheila had encouraged the managers to ask.

Despite these limitations, Sheila wants to make it clear that the new law doesn't prevent her managers from searching public sources for information about applicants. There's nothing wrong with managers doing an Internet search of applicants' names or looking at applicants' public Facebook profiles.

4:02 p.m. Recording Phone Calls and "Intercepting" E-Mails without the Other Party's Consent Is Illegal

Just as Sheila is returning to her office just after 4:00 she hears the phone ring. On the line is Mark Pott, the floor lead from GBI's sales department.

Mark reports that he had been walking around the sales department making sure everything was in order when he noticed an amused crowd gathered around Julie Brown's desk. Julie had a big smile on her face and her cellphone up to the earpiece of her landline. Mark signaled for the crowd to disburse and asked Julie what was going on. Julie quickly hung up the phone and then admitted to using her cellphone to record a customer's voice, then speeding up the voice with an app, and replaying the recording for the audience around her.

Mark found Julie's conduct to be inappropriate and wants Sheila's take on whether the conduct warrants discipline. "It most definitely does," says Sheila. "Not only was Julie rude to that customer, but what she did may be illegal."

Sheila explains to Mark that California has a strict eavesdropping law in which a party cannot intercept or record a telephone conversation unless everyone on the phone consents to the recording. Therefore, to monitor calls without violating California law, GBI must notify the employee *and* the customer that his or her calls may be monitored. In contrast, in some states and at the federal level, eavesdropping is only illegal if neither party on the phone is aware of the monitoring/recording. In those jurisdictions, it's OK to record a call as long as one party on the phone consents to the recording.

In this case, Julie conducted the recording without the customer's consent. And unlike the phone lines in GBI's customer service department, on which a prerecorded message warns customers that their "call may be monitored or recorded for quality assurance purposes," GBI does not insert a disclaimer on calls made to the sales department.

If the customer that Julie recorded were to find out, the customer could claim that Julie acted "maliciously, and without consent," which is a criminal act. Not only did Julie expose herself to criminal liability for recording the phone call, but she put the company at risk for civil liability.

This incident reminds Sheila of GBI's aborted attempt to institute an e-mail "filtering" program to intercept e-mails from employees. The system had been designed to monitor e-mails mid-transmission to ensure that they complied with GBI's communication guidelines and customer service standards. GBI's legal department advised against intercepting e-mails, however, because the practice could violate eavesdropping prohibitions. The lawyers explained that the rules for monitoring e-mail communications are governed by the same principles as telephone conversations.

Under both federal and state law, an employer may generally inspect e-mails that are "stored" on the employer's network as long as the employer has a legitimate interest in viewing the communication and the employee doesn't have a reasonable expectation of privacy while using his or her work e-mail. But employers cannot intercept e-mails mid-transmission unless they first obtain consent. Therefore, unless GBI provided notice to the employee and to all other senders and recipients of the e-mail, it could face liability for intercepting an e-mail mid-transmission. If GBI were located outside California and subject only to federal law, there would be no need for the other party or parties to consent to the interception; the employee's consent would be sufficient to validate the interception of the e-mail.

5:56 p.m. California's Discrimination Laws Prohibit Discrimination for Breast-Feeding

It's just about 6:00 p.m. and Sheila is back in her office trying to get through her e-mails. She went from 12 e-mails at 7:30 a.m. this morning to 36 e-mails now. She looks up and catches the eye of Josh Meeks, the customer service manager, walking by, Josh pivots and comes to her door.

Josh tells Sheila that Carrie Farid, a mother who recently returned from maternity leave, is locking the break room twice a day for 25 minutes to express milk for her newborn baby. Josh says he's "disgusted" by Carrie's taking out her breast where he eats. Plus, he says, "Carrie's long breaks are killing my department's productivity." Josh also doesn't see why Carrie can't just stay home until she's done breast-feeding.

Sheila is taken aback. First of all, she explains, federal and state laws require the company to make reasonable efforts to provide nursing mothers with the use of a room or other location (other than a toilet stall) to express milk in private. These same laws also require companies to provide breast-feeding mothers with a reasonable amount of break time to express their milk, except where providing extra break time would "seriously" hinder the employer's operations.

Sheila goes on, "Is the break room really an appropriate place for her to nurse? It would be OK if we had no place else, but I think we have options that would be much more private. Also, the California legislature just passed legislation prohibiting discrimination against nursing mothers. I'm concerned that your comments could be construed as discriminatory against Carrie's status as a breast-feeding mother."

Sheila urges Josh to be more understanding, and they quickly begin searching the building for a better location for Carrie to express milk going forward. Sheila also makes a mental note to check up on Carrie from time to time, given Josh's comments.

After Josh leaves for the night, Sheila's mind continues to linger on his comments. GBI takes discrimination and harassment very seriously, and for good reason. The California FEHA requires employers to take all reasonable steps to prevent discrimination and harassment from occurring in the workplace. In the 2003 case *American Airlines v. Superior Court (DiMarco)*, a California Court of Appeal interpreted that to mean that employers have an affirmative duty to conduct a prompt investigation of discrimination and retaliation claims. Federal EEOC guidance also urges employers to complete thorough investigations of such claims.

If Josh doesn't heed Sheila's warning, and Carrie complains that Josh is discriminating against her or harassing her based on a protected characteristic, Sheila will have no choice but to launch an investigation.

8:15 p.m. California Employers Must Be Careful (and Honest) When Providing Job References Based on Performance

It's 8:15 p.m. and Sheila is hungry. She's been at work for almost 13 hours. Before she goes home, however, Sheila opens one last e-mail. The e-mail is from her HR counterpart at GBI's fiercest rival, Marla from Left Coast Industries. Marla and Sheila get along remarkably well given that their employers are in competition.

Dear Sheila,

I hope this e-mail finds you well. I am writing because we just received an application from one of your former employees, John Mason. Given his long tenure, I would appreciate your thoughts on Mr. Mason's work ethic and capabilities. Please call or e-mail me at your convenience.

Marla

Reference requests are always challenging for Sheila because, as an HR professional, Sheila relies heavily on the valuable information past employers provide about employees. But GBI's lawyers have strongly discouraged the company from sharing performance information with prospective employers. Sheila has been instructed to limit her responses to objective criteria such as dates of employment and earnings.

This advice is difficult for Sheila to understand given that California Civil Code Section 47 seems to provide protections for employers that make statements based on "credible evidence" in response to a prospective employer's request for job performance and qualification information. Even so, GBI's lawyers have explained to Sheila that statements by past employers lose their privileged status if it's found that the statements were made with malice.

Therefore, regardless of Sheila's honesty or intentions, if a former employee is upset about a recommendation and tends to be litigious, one offhand comment could get the company sued on what is a completely bogus defamation claim.

> Dear Marla,
>
> Thank you for your e-mail. In response to your inquiry about Mr. Mason, our records show that he worked for GBI from April 11, 2006, until July 17, 2012. My records also show that Mr. Mason's hourly rate on the date he was hired was $26.42 and that his hourly rate at his termination was $32.67/hour.
>
> It's been a long day for me. Hopefully your day has been a little less grueling.
>
> Sheila

This prompts the reply:

> Dear Sheila,
>
> I get it—name, rank & serial number. Thanks for your "help."
> Of course, I can't be too mad. I'd have done the same thing to you. ☺
>
> Marla

Sheila smiles tiredly. She looks at the clock. It's now 8:47 p.m. She says to herself, "At least rush hour will be over by now . . . I hope."

Epilogue

Los Angeles, August 2012

"You mean it's finally over?", the VP-HR asked me, her sense of relief palpable, even over a phone line from 2,000 miles away.

"Yep," I said. "We got back the signed release agreement this morning. The dismissal should be filed tomorrow, and as soon as you send me the settlement checks, I'll have them delivered to opposing counsel."

"I still can't believe we got this resolved so quickly," the GC said. "I had the board ready for a two-year fight."

It turned out that, despite all the sound and fury from the plaintiff's attorney before the start of the case, the facts really were in my client's favor. The plaintiff, a disgruntled former salesperson who was fired for repeatedly missing work, had claimed a variety of disability and leave-law violations, but when pushed, was not able to back up the claims with any doctor's notes. Ultimately, after six months of discovery and a few depositions, the worst the plaintiff could accuse my client of was failing to sit down and discuss what accommodations might exist for his nonexistent disability. (Yes, California law really does allow someone to sue a company for failing to talk about an accommodation for a nonexistent disability.)

Though it was entirely possible that we could have convinced the court to dismiss the case before trial, the time and expense involved in doing so (plus the inherent uncertainty of never knowing how a judge would rule) would have been significantly more than the amount for which the plaintiff ended up settling the case. The VP-HR had to make a business decision—pay my firm a lot to likely win, or pay the plaintiff substantially less to go away and never come back. I cannot blame the company for the choice it made … even though it would have been a fun case to try.

⚖️ ⚖️ ⚖️

What my client learned during that relatively short eight months of litigation is that, even in California, nothing beats good facts when it comes to employment litigation. Even though the state's employment laws increase the cost of doing business and make litigation practically inevitable, having HR and management teams that know what records to keep, what questions to ask (or not ask), and what policies to follow can really give a company an advantage.

I hope that this book helps give you that advantage. California is a beautiful state—I grew up there, and now have had the pleasure of practicing law there. Businesses can make a lot of money operating there. But that beauty comes at a cost. You have to decide whether it's a cost worth paying. Many think it is; some not. But if you're willing to take a chance on the Golden State, it's best to come prepared.

Now that I have moved in-house and head the employment law practice for one of my former clients—one that does significant business in California—I am more grateful than ever for my time spent in California. It is a constant challenge to keep up on the ever-shifting standards, but well worth it for any company that wants to take advantage of the benefits California has to offer.

Appendix A:
Citations and Sources

The order of the entries is organized by the order in which they appearing in each chapter.

Chapter 1

The complete set of Wage Orders is available at http://www.dir.ca.gov/iwc/wageorderindustries.htm.

The Department of Labor Standards Enforcement (DLSE) has published a useful guide with an index of business and occupations and their corresponding Wage Orders: *Which IWC Order?*, available at http://www.dir.ca.gov/dlse/WhichIWCOrderClassifications.PDF.

Chapter 2

Labrie v. UPS Supply Chain Solutions, Inc., 2009 WL 4196590 (N.D. Cal. 2009).

Hasty v. Electronic Arts, 2006 WL 134723 (Cal. Superior 2006).

Chapter 3

The Fair Employment and Housing Act (FEHA) is codified at California Government Code §§ 12900-12996.

Macy v. Holder, Appeal No. 0120120821 (U.S. Equal Employment Opportunity Commission, April 20, 2012).

Department of Fair Employment & Housing v. Acosta Tacos, FEHC Dec. No. 09-03-P, 2009 WL 2595487 (Cal.F.E.H.C.) filed June 19, 2009.

Hazen Paper Co. v. Biggins, 507 U.S. 604, 611 (1993).

Reese v. Barton Healthcare Systems, 693 F.Supp.2d 1170 (E.D.Cal., 2010).

Roby v. McKesson, 47 Cal.4th 686, 219 P.3d 749 (Cal., 2009).

San Francisco Police Code § 3303.

Santa Cruz Municipal Code § 9.83.010.

San Diego Human Dignity Ordinance, Chap. 5, Art. 2, Div. 96.

Chapter 4

Family and Medical Leave Act (FMLA), 29 U.S.C. § 2612 et seq.

Uniformed Services Employment and Reemployment Rights Act (USERRA), 38 U.S.C. § 4301 et seq.

California Family Rights Act (CFRA), California Gov. C. § 12945.2 et seq.

Pregnancy Disability Leave Law (PDLL), California Gov. C. § 12945 et seq.

Paid Family Leave (PFL), Unemp. Ins. C. §§ 2601, 3301 et seq.; see also 22 C.C.R. § 3303-1;

Kin Care Leave, California Labor Code § 233.

Domestic Violence and Sexual Assault Victims Leave, Labor Code § 230.1.

Crime Victims Leave, California Labor Code § 230.2.

Emergency Duties Leave Laws, California Labor Code §§ 230.3 and 230.4.

Family School Partnership Act, California Labor Code § 230.8.

"Time Off to Vote" Law, California Elections Code §§ 14000-14003.

CAP Leave, California Labor Code §§ 1500 to 1507.

Organ and Bone Marrow Leave Law, California Labor Code § 1510 et seq.

Sanchez v. Swissport, Inc., Docket Number B237761, California Court of Appeals, Second District (February 21, 2013).

Chapter 5

California Constitution Article 1.

California Business and Profession Code § 16600.

California Civil Code § 47.

California Code of Civil Procedure § 527.3 (Moscone Act).

California Education Code § 72330.5.

California Education Code § 87013.

California Fair Employment and Housing Act, California Government Code § 12940 et. seq.

California Health and Safety Code § 11362.785.

California Labor Code § 226(c).

California Labor Code § 432.7.

California Labor Code § 432.8.

California Labor Code § 980.

California Labor Code § 1174.

California Labor Code § 1197.5.

California Labor Code § 1299.

Title VII of the Civil Rights Act of 1964, 42 U.S.C. § 2000e et seq.

American Airlines v. Superior Court (DiMarco), 114 Cal.App.4th 881 (2003).

Ralphs Grocery Company v. United Food and Commercial Workers Union, Local 8, Cal.4th 186 Cal.App.4th 1078 (2010).

Appendix B:
Additional Laws of Note

This book covers many of the most common employment laws from the state of California, but there are a few others that, due to size constraints, I was not able to address. The following laws are directly relevant to most businesses, and I encourage you to review the website listed for additional information on them, or to contact your labor and employment attorney for guidance.

Workplace Safety

The Division of Occupational Safety and Health (known as Cal/OSHA) is the California counterpart to the federal Occupational Safety and Health Administration (OSHA) and is responsible for protecting workers and the public from workplace safety hazards. Information on Cal/OSHA and its efforts can be found at http://www.dir.ca.gov/dosh/. Information on the federal OSHA can be found at http://www.osha.gov/.

Business Closings

The federal Worker Adjustment and Retraining Notification (WARN) Act requires most employers with 100 or more employees to provide notification 60 calendar days in advance of plant closings and mass layoffs. Administered by the U.S. Department of Labor, information on the WARN Act can be found at http://www.dol.gov/compliance/laws/comp-warn.htm. California has its own version of WARN, Cal-WARN. Information on Cal-WARN can be found at http://www.dir.ca.gov/dlse/Cal-WARNAct.html.

Anti-Human Trafficking

On January 1, 2012, the California Transparency in Supply Chains Act of 2010 went into effect. Essentially a disclosure law, it requires certain large companies (retail sellers or manufacturers with at least

$100,000,000 in worldwide gross receipts) to make certain representations concerning the businesses' efforts to combat and eradicate human trafficking. Compliance with the law is not difficult, but does require certain specific efforts regarding disclosure to be made. The full text of the law can be found at: http://leginfo.legislature.ca.gov/faces/billNav Client.xhtml?bill_id=200920100SB657&search_keywords=.

⚖ ⚖ ⚖

Details about these and, quite frankly, all the laws, rules, and regulations discussed in this book can be found in the excellent book (written by my former partner Doug Farmer from Ogletree's San Francisco office): *California Employment Law: The Complete Survival Guide to Doing Business in California*, available at the SHRMStore (www.shrmstore. shrm.org). It is a wonderful resource for any company based or doing business in California.

Index

Acknowledgements

I want to thank Becca Polak, General Counsel for KAR Auction Services, Inc., who allowed me to complete this project after my move from Ogletree Deakins to the wonderful in-house life at KAR. Thanks also go to Ogletree Deakins' Managing Shareholder Kim Ebert and the rest of the Ogletree board of directors for embracing the idea of this book series, and to Jathan Janove, for entrusting me with one of the first products.

I also want to thank Ogletree attorneys Kimberly Carter, Owen Dallmeyer, Jean Kosela, John Migliarini, and Alex Santana for all their hard work on helping me with the copious details in this book. They helped me get it right. To the extent there are any errors, they are mine alone.

Finally, I want to offer a very heartfelt thank you to all the Ogletree attorneys from California, who put up with me during the painful learning process as I acclimated to practicing law in the Golden State.

About the Author

Matthew S. Effland is the Vice President-Employment Law, for KAR Auction Services, Inc. Prior to starting his in-house career, he was a shareholder in the Indianapolis office of Ogletree Deakins law firm, as well as the former managing shareholder for Ogletree's Los Angeles office.

About Ogletree Deakins

Ogletree Deakins is one of the largest labor and employment law firms representing management in all types of employment-related legal matters. The firm has 700 lawyers located in 45 offices across the United States and in Europe.

Ogletree Deakins is the "Law Firm of the Year" in both the Employment Law—Management and Labor Law—Management categories in the 2014 edition of the *U.S. News—Best Lawyers®* "Best Law Firms" list.

Ogletree Deakins was awarded the Starbucks Law & Corporate Affairs Excellence in Diversity Award for 2013. The prestigious award recognizes the diversity efforts of Ogletree Deakins, including diversity metrics within the firm's lawyer population, participation in professional diversity events, pipeline support, retention, organizational structure to support diversity, and overall commitment to diversity.

In addition to handling labor and employment law matters, the firm has thriving practices focused on business immigration, employee benefits, and workplace safety and health law. Ogletree Deakins represents a diverse range of clients, from small businesses to *Fortune* 50 companies. To learn more, visit http://www.ogletreedeakins.com.

Additional SHRM-Published Books

101 Sample Write Ups for Documenting Employee Performance Problems: A Guide to Progressive Discipline & Termination
Paul Falcone

57 Frequently Asked Questions About Workplace Safety and Security: With Answers from SHRM's Knowledge Advisors
Edited by Margaret Fiester

97 Frequently Asked Questions About Compensation: With Answers from SHRM's Knowledge Advisors
Edited by Margaret Fiester

The Essential Guide to Federal Employment Laws
Lisa Guerin and Amy DelPo

The Essential Guide to Workplace Investigations: How to Handle Employee Complaints & Problems
Lisa Guerin

From Hello to Goodbye: Proactive Tips for Maintaining Positive Employee Relations
Christine V. Walters

The Legal Context of Staffing
Jean M. Phillips Stanley M. Gully

The Manager's Guide to HR: Hiring, Firing, Performance Evaluations, Documentation, Benefits, and Everything Else You Need to Know
Max Muller

Stop Bullying at Work: Strategies and Tools for HR and Legal Professionals
Teresa A. Daniel